Soundings

Issue 32

Bare
Life

Founding Editors
Stuart Hall
Doreen Massey
Michael Rustin

Editor
Jonathan Rutherford

Managing Editor
Sally Davison

Associate Editors
Geoff Andrews
Sarah Benton

Reviews Editor
Jo Littler

Art Editor
Tim Davison

Editorial Office
Lawrence & Wishart
99a Wallis Road
London E9 5LN

Advertisements
Write for information to
Soundings,
c/o Lawrence & Wishart

Subscriptions
2006 subscription rates are (for three issues):
UK: Institutions £80, Individuals £35
Rest of the world: Institutions £90, Individuals £45

ISSN 1362 6620
ISBN 1-905007-37-X

Printed in Great Britain by
Cambridge University Press, Cambridge

Soundings is published three times a year, in
autumn, spring and summer by:
Lawrence & Wishart,
99a Wallis Road, London E9 5LN.
Email: soundings@lwbks.co.uk

Website: www.lwbooks.co.uk/journals/soundings/contents.html

CONTENTS

———————————— Continued on next page ————————————

Soundings

is now *freely* available *online* to all subscribers

Benefits include:

♦ Document to document linking using live references, for fast,
   reliable access to wider, related literature.
♦ Journal content that is fully searchable, across full text, abstracts,
   titles, TOCs and figures.
♦ Live links to and from major Abstract and Indexing resources to
   aid research.
♦ The ability to conduct full-text searching across multiple
   journals, giving you a wider view of the research that counts.
♦ Powerful TOC alerting services that keep you up to date with the
   latest research.

Set up access now at: www.ingentaselect.com/register.htm
and follow the online instructions*

Subscription Enquiries: help@ingenta.com

*Access is provided by Ingenta Select, an Ingenta website

NOTES ON CONTRIBUTORS

Jon Baldwin is Senior Lecturer in Communications at the London Metropolitan University. He is co-editor of *Subject Matters* and *Film-Philosophy*.

Tony Bennett is Professor of Sociology at the Open University, where is also Director of the ESRC Centre for Research on Socio-Cultural Change, jointly managed with the University of Manchester.

Suresh Parshottamdas Dalal was born in 1932 in Mumbai. He set up the publishing company Image Publications and Writings to promote Gujarati literary and cultural life. He edits the Gujarati poetry journal *Kavita* and the literary quarterly *Vivecana*. He is the recipient of many literary awards including five Gujarat Government Awards for his contribution to Gujarati literature.

Joolz Denby is an award-winning writer, photographer and illustrator. Her novel *Stone Baby* won the New Crime Writer of the Year award and the USA Earphone Award. *Billie Morgan* was short-listed for the Orange Prize 2005. Joolz has published four collections of poetry and short stories. Visit www.joolz.net for further information.

Faisal Devji is Assistant Professor of History at the New School University, New York. His book on the role of militancy and morality in the globalisation of Islam is *Landscapes of the Jihad: Militancy, Morality, Modernity* (Hurst 2005).

Pat Devine is an Honorary Research Fellow in the School of Social Sciences at the University of Manchester. He is currently writing a book on the political economy of a post-capitalist society.

Kurt Jacobsen, author or editor of six books, is a journalist and research associate in the Political Science Department of the University of Chicago.

Sayeed Khan is a freelance journalist, political activist and writer on South Asian affairs. He lectures at Pavia and Bologna universities in Italy.

Ruth Lister is Professor of Social Policy at Loughborough University. She is a former Director of the Child Poverty Action Group and is a member of the Fabian Commission on Life Chances and Child Poverty. Her latest book is *Poverty* (Polity 2004).

Doreen Massey is a founding editor of *Soundings*.

Richard Minns is an independent researcher based in Argentina, and visiting research fellow at the University of Sheffield. He is author of *The Cold War in Welfare: Stock Markets versus Pensions* (Verso 2001).

Janet Newman is Professor of Social Policy at the Open University.

Michael Rustin is a founding editor of *Soundings*.

Jonathan Rutherford is editor of *Soundings*.

Carole Satyamurti was formerly poetry editor of *Soundings*. Her latest book is *Stitching The Dark: New & Selected Poems*, Bloodaxe Books 2005.

Ejos Ubiribo is a freelance writer, cultural commentator and a member of Trident Independent Advisory Group (IAG), which provides Trident Operation Command Unit (OCU) with independent advice in tackling gun crime, interaction with and the policing of the black communities in London. She has contributed to many pro-active anti-gun crime initiatives engaging with 'at risk' youth to divert them from criminality, and energetically works/ lobbies for the empowerment of disaffected members of her community.

Robin Wilson has been director of the Belfast-based think tank Democratic Dialogue since he founded it in the wake of the paramilitary ceasefires in Northern Ireland in 1994. He was formerly editor of *Fortnight* magazine and is a regular contributor to the British, Irish and international media on Northern Ireland affairs. He chairs the policy committee of the Northern Ireland Community Relations Council and is an adviser to the Council of Europe programme on intercultural dialogue and conflict prevention.

C. K. Williams's most recent book, *The Singing*, won the National Book Award for 2003; his previous book, *Repair*, was awarded the 2000 Pulitzer Prize; and in 2005 he was awarded the Ruth Lilly Poetry Prize. His *Collected Poems* will appear in November 2006. He teaches in the Creative Writing Program at Princeton University.

Bare life

'Bare life' - or mere life - is a phrase that has recently been brought into debate by Giorgio Agamben.[1] It is used to signal a contrast between mere biological life and human life as cultural, political and civic. This distinction raises many questions about what it means to be - and to be recognised as - fully human.

In the enlightenment tradition, citizenship of a nation state implies rights, recognition, membership of a legitimate collectivity. The concept of human rights, though ostensibly a universal term, is closely connected to this idea; it is underpinned by quite complex ideas about what constitutes membership of humanity. As neoliberal globalisation intensifies some of these underpinnings are beginning to unravel. Nation states are less powerful; millions live beyond the protection of states, whether as internally displaced people or as refugees; and an increasing number of countries are regarded as failed states or rogue states. Alongside these developments, the United States has adopted a much more interventionist global stance in recent years. Its promotion of global markets has become infused with a revived sense of its mission to spread 'civilisation' to what it increasingly sees as barbarian badlands (see Jonathan Rutherford's commentary in this issue for more on this). All this is very bad news for the large proportion of the world's population that is at risk of slipping into a condition of 'mere life'.

In this issue, several contributors discuss terror and the 'war' against it. Faisal Devji focuses on Al-Qaeda, which, he argues, is itself the product of globalisation. He sees parallels between Al-Qaeda and other global movements, all of which have no forum in which they can have political purchase. This means that their politics is based on ethics and identity, rather than taking the form of a political organisation that is focused on transforming a state. He also shows how Al-Qaeda flourishes in the interstices of the global marketplace -

---

1. See Giorgio Agamben, *'Form-of-life'*, *Means Without End*, University of Minnesota Press. The term 'mere life' comes from the work of Walter Benjamin - see 'Critique of Violence' in *One Way Street and Other Writings*, Verso 1985. For a discussion of bare life in relation to asylum seekers, see also Nira Yuval Davis, 'Human security and asylum seeking', *Mediactive 4 Asylum*.

its existence is dependent on the global mobility of people and money. This is a movement that is dissolving traditional Islamic politics - hence its appeal to the young. Faisal Devji's approach is interesting because it treats Al-Qaeda as a political response to world events, rather than as a monster besieging the gates of civilisation.

Kurt Jacobsen documents the rise and rise of the rehabilitation of the strategy of 'pacification' in the United States. He traces the continuities between the pacification of the wild west and modern day military strategy. He shows how this policy failed totally in Vietnam - mainly because of the huge contradiction between winning hearts and minds (which is theoretically part of the strategy) and bombing and napalming people. An outside state's model of civilisation - however defined - is not something that can be violently imposed on another country. Violent imposition is predicated on a refusal to give credence to the standpoint of those who oppose you; it stems from regarding your opponent as less than fully human. And, as Mike Rustin shows in his discussion of Robert McNamara's recent recantations, this is an unlikely pathway to conflict resolution - and hence to any real peace.

Sayeed Khan looks at the history of Afghanistan in the last century and a half. He shows how successive attempts at imposed 'modernisation' have resulted in the entrenchment of conservatism. The polarisations of the cold war then led the West to side with the mujahidin, with tragic and destabilising consequences for the region. The attempt to defend against the encroachments of the old communist enemy have helped to give birth to something even more frightening.

Doreen Massey identifies the beast that is driving so much of this agenda. She reminds us that it is important not to think of globalisation as something that always arrives from somewhere else. In her discussion of the GLA's London Plan, she draws attention to the fact that London - especially the City of London - is a main site in the *production* of neoliberal globalisation. This means that when we celebrate diversity, we should not forget the external effects of London's position as a world city (and this argument is generalisable to other global centres). We need to contest this aspect of London's role much more actively.

Many of those who live within the walls of civilisation also experience less than full recognition of their humanity. Ejos Ubiribo's moving contribution shows the pain that fuels the gun crime epidemic among some subcultures of young black men in Britain. Through her dialogues with people involved in this life, she succeeds in conveying the sense of exclusion that drives people to try to seize their own version of the good life (money and respect - as in the mainstream) through violence. That this is a strategy borne of desperation can be seen in the death and destruction it has brought to so many.

Ruth Lister also draws attention to a key flaw in New Labour's 'respect agenda'; it has completely overlooked the lack of recognition and respect from dominant groups in society towards those who live in poverty. In pointing to the many exclusions experienced by those living on low incomes - from consumption, from recognition, from power, from dignity - she calls for the respect agenda to be turned upside down.

Elsewhere in the issue, Robin Wilson argues that making concessions to communalism, as in the Belfast Agreement of 1998, is no solution to inter-ethnic conflict. Instead he calls for a politics based on more fluid conceptions of identity and a civic cosmopolitanism. Richard Minns discusses the gradual transformation of the Israeli state - once firmly anchored in a corporatist Labour Zionism, it has now adapted itself to the neoliberal norm. These changes are analysed through the prism of what is going on in pension funds - institutions that are hugely important both financially and socially, and are consequently excellent barometers of wider attitudes.

Pat Devine argues that after the falling apart of the postwar settlement in 1970s, a move towards neoliberalism was not inevitable. The political history of this period, as well as alternatives put forward by the left at that time, is worth revisiting, since we are still living with the consequences of the reverses we suffered then.

Finally, Janet Newman offers some interesting reflections on competing ideas about the nature of the public and the different terrains across which battles are currently being fought. The retreat of the public under the onslaught of the market is another process which has been underway since the 1970s, and here too, as Janet argues, it is important to go beyond social democratic conceptions of the public sphere if we are to make a serious challenge to creeping marketisation.

The world without light

Jonathan Rutherford

On 11 September 2001 I was part of a crowd that had gathered round a shop window to watch the World Trade Centre burning. When United Airlines Flight 175 crashed into the south tower I felt the symbolic order of the world I'd grown up in reverberate in shock. In the days that followed I experienced a nostalgia for the TV-created America of my 1960s childhood. I recalled the programmes of small-town, homespun innocence fringed with the threat of disorder that had played such an important part in shaping my cultural imagination. The bloody borders of the American imperium with their torturing of enemies by proxies, the crushing economic exploitation and overthrowing of uncooperative governments were transmogrified into the TV and cinematic images of the mythic Western frontier in which the Indians bloodlessly bit the dust. In this celluloid Wild West, the military fort established in frontier country followed in the wake of the hunter and trader, consolidating US military power, securing markets and delivering white civilisation to the 'hostiles'. After 11 September large swathes of the world became 'injun country'.

'This is civilization's fight'

In his January 2002 State of the Union address, President Bush spelt out his imperial mission. It contained three essential elements: 'active American global leadership' - the entire world is the battlefield and the enemy will be pursued wherever they are; 'regime change' - terrorist organisations *and* rogue regimes are targets in the war on terrorism; and 'promoting liberal democratic principles' - no nation will be exempt from the 'non-negotiable demands' of liberty, law and justice.[1] Like the Cheyenne military culture of the nineteenth century, Al-Qaeda assailed the American imagination with its fabled devotion to spiritual violence and its embracing of death. Richard Myers, chairman of the Joint Chiefs of Staff, described the threat: 'These folks are savages, mass murderers'. Donald Rumsfeld was more expansive. The enemy comes from a world that is pre-modern: 'They combine medieval views with modern tools and technologies. They operate within hostile and friendly nation-states and even within our own country'. A *Business Week* editorial (20.9.04) announced that, 'a new age of barbarism is upon us'. The terrorists have but one demand, 'the destruction of modern secular society'.

Osama bin Laden, in his 1996 'Declaration of War against the Americans Occupying the Land of the Two Holy Places', announced his fatwa with these opening words: 'Our youths believe in paradise after death. They believe that taking part in fighting will not bring their day nearer; and staying behind will not postpone their day either.'[2] Bin Laden confronted the West with its fear of death: 'Those youths are different from your soldiers. Your problem will be how to convince your troops to fight'. In Ridley Scott's *Black Hawk Down*, a film whose unspoken message is the moral righteousness of the American imperial mission, Somali militia men are all linked into the same nihilistic embrace of death. One tells a captured American helicopter pilot: 'In Somalia killing is negotiation. There will always be killing, you see. This is the way things are in our world'. The imaginary of the Global War on Terror has created a fragmenting world of chaos, inhumanity and unrestrained hatred. Mogadishu is depicted as a bankrupted Dantean inferno, teeming with armed black multitudes driven solely by the desire to kill Americans. Here is the dark abyss beyond the borders of the American imperium - the lands without light, literally.

P.H. Liotta and James Miskel, two academics at the influential US Naval War College, use this metaphor of darkness to describe the new world order confronting America. In their 'Redrawing the Map of the Future' they

---

1. Gary Schmitt, Tom Donnelly, 'Memorandum to Opinions Leaders "The Bush Doctrine"',www.newamericancentury.org/defense-20020130.htm, 30.1.02.
2. Osama bin Laden, 'Declaration of War against the Americans Occupying the Land of the Two Holy Places', www.mideastweb.org/osamabinladen1.htm.

reproduce NASA's image of the 'earth at night': flows and grids of light punctuate the azure of the earth's surface, identifying the areas of economic development.[3] Their interest in this photograph lies in the pockets of darkness - the Caribbean Rim, virtually all of Africa, the Balkans, the Caucasus, Central Asia, the Middle East, Southwest Asia and much of Southeast Asia. These are lands which have been excluded from global flows of trade and capital, where soon half the population will be aged 15-29 and without employment or educational opportunities. Here, they write, are the 'feral zones' of under-governed remote rural areas, the semi-urbanised collections of displaced populations, the 'bubbling petri dishes' of the new arc of mega slum cities - Lagos-Cairo-Karachi-Jakarta - and the militia run 'para-states' which behave like zombies kept alive by injections of aid. In these places, they argue, lie the future threats to the United States. Their solution is a marketised version of Bush's imperial mission. Intervene politically and economically and connect up these areas to the global economy: 'If September 11 taught us anything, it is that our security is inextricably connected to domestic governance shortcomings elsewhere.'

The military-market complex

For some, markets are enough to lighten the darkness. Liotta and Miskell's prescription for the Global War on Terror has its origins in the Clinton Presidency of the 1990s. Clinton's priority of opening up markets in East Asia, creating the North American Free Trade Area (NAFTA), and supporting the setting up of the World Trade Organisation, was a major force behind the growth of globalisation. Samuel Bodman, then Deputy Secretary of the US Department of Commerce, explained the strategy: 'The US economy is in recession, and our goal is to get America working again. The United States sorely needs the stimulus of trade ... Furthermore, it is evident that our security at home is inextricably linked to the security and stability of nations across the world.'[4] Charles Krauthammer, in his famous essay describing the 'unipolar moment' of US global

---

3. P.H. Liotta and James F. Miskel, 'Redrawing the Map of the Future', *World Policy Journal*, March, 2004, www.worldpolicy.org/journal/articles/wpj04-1/Liotta.pdf.
4. Remarks of Deputy Secretary Samuel Bodman, at the 'Services 2002 Conference', A Business-Government Dialogue on US Trade Expansion Objectives, US Department of Commerce, 5.2.02, www.uscsi.org, www.uscsi.org.

hegemony, was less circumspect: 'America's involvement abroad is in many ways an essential pillar of the American economy.'[5] US policy has been an ambiguous relationship between brute self interest and the ideological belief that globalised capitalism will civilise the world. Under the Bush administration, the link between trade and security has increased exponentially with its policy of 'competitive liberalization'. His strategy attempts to tie together US military and corporate interests in regional and bilateral Free Trade Agreements (FTAs). In May 2003, he announced plans to create a US-Middle East Free Trade Agreement by 2013. Robert Zoellick, US Representative of Trade at the time, told an audience at the World Economic Forum in Jordan: 'Our trade agenda is a fundamental part of the President's broader Middle East initiative ... Our goal is to assist nations that are ready to embrace economic liberty and the rule of law, integrate into the global trading system, and bring their economies into the modern era.'

The role of markets in the War on Terror has been most forthrightly championed by Thomas P.M. Barnett, a former researcher with the Centre for Naval Analyses (and a Democrat). After 9/11 he became Assistant for Strategic Futures in the Pentagon's Office of Force Transformation, an initiative set up by Donald Rumsfeld to carry through the comprehensive restructuring of the US military (the Revolution in Military Affairs). Barnett's proposals for military strategy are directly linked to his belief in the civilising mission of capitalism. Like Liotta and Miskell, Barnett identifies the limits of globalisation as a key factor in US security:

> Show me where globalization is thick with network connectivity, financial transactions, liberal media flows, and collective security, and I will show you regions featuring stable governments, rising standards of living, and more deaths by suicide than murder ... These parts of the world I call the Functioning Core, or Core ... But show me where globalization is thinning or just plain absent, and I will show you regions plagued by politically repressive regimes, widespread poverty and disease, routine mass murder, and - most important - the chronic conflicts that incubate the next generation of global terrorists ... These parts of the world I call the Non-Integrating Gap, or Gap.[6]

---

5. Charles Krauthammer, 'The Unipolar Moment', *Foreign Affairs* 70, 1991, p27.
6. T. Barnett, 'The Pentagon's New Map', *Esquire*, March, 2003.

According to Barnett, the United States faces three tasks. First, it must 'bolster the Core's immune-system response' to 'disruptive perturbations' unleashed by events like 9/11. Second, it has to build a 'firewall' against Gap exports of 'terror, drugs, pandemics'. 'Seam states' that lie along the Gap's 'bloody boundaries' must be targeted: Mexico, Brazil, South Africa, Morocco, Algeria, Greece, Turkey, Pakistan, Thailand, Malaysia, the Philippines, and Indonesia. Third it must steadily increase the export of security to the Gap's worst trouble spots. Military bases should be positioned permanently within the Gap: there are no exit strategies.[7]

Barnett's world is polarised into a threatening, uncivilised outside and a civilised inside that needs defending. The market is the means by which the civilised inside can be extended. He believes that victories in the War on Terror will be won by the private sector, not by the state or the military: 'we don't need business to "get behind the war", but to get out in front of it.'[8] Bases will follow emerging markets in order to consolidate US geopolitical dominance. In 2001, Barnett worked with the investment bank Cantor Fitzgerald to map out future relations between commerce and the military. His 'New Rules Set Project' identified a military-market complex that will facilitate a steady rise of connectivity between national economies. Inward flows of private capital investment will utilise the 'inexpensive but dependable labor' of Gap countries. In turn they must develop 'good governance' and the enforcement of property rights and contracts. Barnett offers the example of Asia. In Asia, the commander-in-chief of US Pacific Command guarantees the security of the region. 'We trade little pieces of paper (our currency, in the form of a trade deficit) for Asia's amazing array of products and services. We are smart enough to know this is a patently unfair deal unless we offer something of great value along with those little pieces of paper. That product is a strong US Pacific Fleet, which squares the transaction nicely.'[9]

Barnett's faith in an American imperial destiny, with the US acting as global moral compass and exporter of security, requires the naive assumption that its

7. T. Barnett, *The Pentagon's New Map*, G.P. Putnam, 2004, p179.
8. T. Barnett, 'The Top Ten Reasons Why I Hate World War IV', *Newsletter from Thomas P.M. Barnett*, 25.4.05, www.thomaspmbarnett.com/weblog.
9. T. Barnett, 'Asia: The Military-Market Link', *The U.S. Naval Institute*, January 2002, www.thomaspmbarnett.com/published/atmml.htm.

economic interests do not conflict with those of other countries. It is in this contradiction that the civilising mission collapses and policing loses any appearance of neutrality. Capital accumulation and the pursuit of profit do not produce the collective, public goods necessary for sustainable and equitable development. Foreign Direct Investment (FDI) does not deal with the root causes of poverty. Market driven globalisation will not reduce the huge, global disparity in wealth. C.P. Chandrasekhar and Jayati Ghosh, in their survey of current global balance of payments, show how the private capital flows that Barnett envisages as creating economic development simply enforce the dependency of peripheral economies on the centre. As they found: 'private capital flowed into developing countries to earn lucrative returns, and this capital then flowed out as investment in low interest Treasury bills in order to finance the US balance of trade deficit.'[10] Korkut Boratav calculates that in 2003 the US economy benefited by up to $428 billions in net resource transfers from the rest of the world.[11] Financial liberalisation conscripts countries into a global financial system in service to the US economy. In the process it reverses the meagre political independence and economic gains made in the process of decolonisation. It's an economics of underdevelopment and it is never going to bring global harmony.

While those who refuse the civilising offer of capitalism place themselves firmly on the outside of world society, some of those within the citadel do particularly well out of the business security link. The War on Terror has enriched many of the corporate friends of the Bush administration. Despite systematic overcharging, Halliburton has won government contracts worth $10.5bn for Operation Iraqi Freedom. The War on Terror is generating huge funds for corporate research and development. The technological sophistication of weaponry, computers and digital technology is a product of the symbiosis between the military and the civilian, high-tech, 'new economy' sector. Companies like Raytheon, Lockheed Martin, L-3 Communications, Alliant Techsystems and DRS Technologies have reconfigured the old military industrial complex that

---

10. C.P. Chandrasekhar & Jayati Ghosh, 'The New Structure of Global Balances', Nov, 2004, networkideas.org/news/nov2004/news11_Global_Balances.htm
11. Korkut Boratav, 'Some Recent Changes on the Relations Between the Metropoles and the Periphery of the Imperialist System', paper presented at the Conference on The Economics of the New Imperialism, New Delhi, January 2004, p5, www.networkideas.org/feathm/feb2004/ft03_IDEAs_Delhi_Conference.htm.

powered mid-twentieth century US technological innovation.

However, the US's role as leviathan is contributing to its budget deficit. The military-market system is effectively financed by foreign creditors, not all of whom share its geopolitical interests. And its dominance in other areas is also being challenged. Its technological lead over China, Brazil and India is narrowing, and these countries are proving difficult to bully and bribe. Bush is finding it hard to persuade them to sign up for Free Trade Agreements - unlike more biddable states such as Chile, Morocco, Bahrain and the Dominican Republic. Samuel Bodman's search for a stimulus to trade as a source of recovery for the US economy remains elusive.

The future

The US has practised a transient form of colonialism. It is unwilling to cast itself as an old-style imperialist, preferring to rely on free-market capitalism as the glue that holds the civilised world together. In its direct interventions, its proponents behave like 'tourists with guns' before returning home and leaving in their wake hybrid borderlands that are more cultural and economic than territorial. (Both Al-Qaeda and the War on Terror are the offspring of these borderlands.) Robert Cooper, a British advocate of liberal imperialism, argues that the barbarism of imperialism belongs to the past. We live in a post-industrial economy dominated by services and an information sector. The state is no longer founded on the principle of violence: 'Hence its unwarlike character. War is essentially a collective activity. In the post-modern state the individual is supreme.' Individual consumption has replaced collective glory as the dominant theme of national life. 'War is to be avoided: empire is of no interest.'[12] This is a variation on the theme of the market state, but it repeats the mistake of ignoring the conflict inherent in capital accumulation.

Contrary to Cooper, though wealthy individuals living in post-industrial societies might be unwilling to sacrifice themselves for the destiny of the nation, there are other means of executing war that can be called on if their way of life is threatened - as it increasingly will be, by global warming and the depletion of oil, gas and water. They will find the resources to police their borders and

---

12. Robert Cooper, *The post-modern state and the world order*, Demos 2000, p31, www.demos.co.uk/catalogue/thepostmodernstate/.

pacify those living on the outside: when there is killing to be done, a partially denationalised protean form of imperialism will find its proxies, mercenaries and private military firms to undertake the necessary dirty work. The military-market complex, to quote from Foucault's telling account of the bio-politics of the modern age, will exercise the power to 'foster life or disallow it to the point of death'. Compliant populations of Barnett's Gap regions will be included where needed in the global labour market. But those who do not play by the rules, or who are simply superfluous (as Zygmunt Bauman has argued in *Wasted Lives*) become, in Walter Benjamin's phrase, 'mere life'. Stripped of their civic status and without recourse to the law and the codes of civility of the state, such peoples can be killed with impunity. 'With mere life', Benjamin writes, 'the rule of law over the living ceases'.[13]

---

13. Walter Benjamin, 'Critique of Violence', *One Way Street and Other Writings*, Verso, 1985, p151.

Al-Qaeda, spectre of globalisation

Faisal Devji

Faisal Devji *argues that Al-Qaeda should be understood as sharing many features with other international movements for social change, largely because it operates, as they do, in a global arena that offers little purchase for traditional politics.*

Like environmentalism, pacifism and other global movements, Al-Qaeda's jihad is concerned with the world as a whole. Just as climatic change or nuclear holocaust are not problems that can be dealt with regionally, but require global attention, so too the jihad's task of gaining justice for Muslims cannot be accomplished piecemeal, and has meaning only at a global level. This is why the whole world must be brought within Al-Qaeda's purview. And Al-Qaeda's violence - ironically - is intimately linked to the connectedness together of all the world's people in a web of mutual obligation and responsibility. It is this web of universal complicity, after all, that allows American or British civilians to be killed in recompense for the killing of Muslims in Iraq. The worldwide web of war spun by Al-Qaeda exists as a kind of spectre of our global inter-relatedness, one that has as yet no specific political form of its own.

Not unlike companies in the world economy, to which they are often compared, participants in the global jihad have neither the ability nor the inclination to control the territories within which they operate. Their relationship with these territories can instead be seen as a series of indirect and speculative investments. Just as with players in the global economy, participants in the jihad are drawn by their investments into a world that does not operate according to their intentions but seems to possess a life of its own. While the attacks of 9/11, for instance, were meticulously planned, they were at the same time completely speculative as far as their effects were concerned, since these could neither be predicted with any degree of certainty, nor controlled in any fashion.

This state of affairs is characteristic of social and oppositional global movements more generally; these are also unable to predict or control the effects of their own actions. These are all movements whose practices are ethical rather than political in nature, because they have been transformed into gestures of risk and duty rather than acts of instrumentality. Like other global movements, the jihad's spectacular demonstrations of strength escape a politics of intentionality and control that is organised around some common history of needs, interests or ideas; they thus create a landscape of relations in which very little, if anything, is shared. So the worldwide mass demonstrations of 2003 protesting the impending war in Iraq were not only the largest global demonstrations yet seen, they also brought together individuals and groups who possessed neither organisational nor ideological commonality of any sort. Like many such movements - for instance Greenpeace - the jihad brings together allies and enemies of the most heterogeneous character, who neither know nor communicate with each other, and who share almost nothing by way of a prior history.

But unlike other forms of global activism, Al-Qaeda's jihad lacks any notion of apocalypse, which is something far more characteristic of Christian and Jewish radicalism, with their talk of the rapture and the end of days, all of which spills over into the apocalyptic imagination of the West's secular movements, such as environmentalism. One could thus argue that the holy war - martyrdom operations and all - is fundamentally about life, while the West it fights appears to be singularly focused on death, even on the annihilation of humanity as a whole: Euro-American cultures are full of concern about every form and manner of disaster, from global warming to weapons of mass destruction. The jihad, however, is worldly and even prosaic; the end it envisioned has nothing supernatural, rapturous or even final about it, and seems indeed to be something of an anti-climax. It gives us no vision of an alternative universe, nor even some revolutionary utopia, only statements about fair trade and democracy.

My argument is that Al-Qaeda's non-apocalyptic stance, and its attention to the prosaic nature of everyday life, forces us to think about its violence in new ways. For one thing, this violence occurs in a world whose concerns are global in dimension and hence resistant to old-fashioned political solutions, thus seeming to call instead for spectacular gestures that are ethical in nature. Such gestures sometimes announce their distance from political rationality by the self-destructive character of their violence. Suicide bombing is the most individualistic of practices, perhaps the only way in which individuality can be exercised in a world that seems to have spun out of control. It is also an ethical gesture that participates only indirectly, if at all, in a solution to the problem it advertises.

As an explicitly ethical enterprise, therefore, the holy war is a highly unstable phenomenon, because its violence derives from the same source as the non-violence of other global networks. Perhaps Al-Qaeda is murderous because it is so unstable, since it is at any moment capable of shifting its practices into those of non-violence. This suggests that violence is not in itself the most important consequence of the jihad. In the long run, violence is probably Al-Qaeda's most superficial and short-lived effect, though it is certainly one of great importance for the moment. Far greater and almost incalculable in its effects is the jihad's democratisation of Islam - accomplished by its fragmentation of traditional forms of religious authority and the dispersal of their elements into a potentially endless series of re-combinations.

Genealogies of Muslim militancy

These possibilities have presented themselves because the jihad has put an end to old-fashioned fundamentalism as a movement dedicated to the establishment of an ideological state. The jihad has replaced what used to be called Islamic fundamentalism at the edge of Muslim militancy. Traditional Muslim militancy had been part and parcel of Cold War politics, and was concerned with the founding through revolution of an ideological state, fashioned in many respects on the communist model that was so popular in Africa and Asia following the Second World War. With the end of the Cold War, however, and the coming into being of a global market for transactions of all kinds, the revolutionary politics whose aim was to institute ideological states quickly began to break down. This sort of fundamentalism, after all, had enjoyed only one success in its many decades of struggle, with the Islamic Republic of Iran.

In order to understand Al-Qaeda's novelty, its jihad must be torn out of the genealogies of political Islam within which it is generally confined. Faced with what is new, and especially what is radically new, the scholar's conservative instinct is always to reach for some genealogy within which this novelty might be anchored and neutralised. In the case of the jihad, this instinct works to place it in the genealogy of something called political Islam, where its ancestry is generally traced to Middle Eastern movements of the modern period like Salafism or Wahhabism.

A curious feature of such genealogies of the jihad is that they all originate in and remain focused specifically upon Sunni Islam and the Middle East, despite the fact that arguably the most successful examples of political Islam have been revolutionary Iran and the Hizbollah in Lebanon, both Shia movements. Among other things, these have contributed to an ostensibly Sunni jihad the language and practice of the 'martyrdom operation', as its suicide attacks are known. Similarly, the fact that the jihad today happens to be based for the most part outside the Middle East (in places like Chechnya, Afghanistan, Pakistan, India and the Philippines), among populations that have barely an inkling of Salafi or Wahhabi traditions, seems to have escaped the notice of scholarly genealogists.

Apparently the very presence of Arab fighters or funding in such places is evidence enough that Salafi or Wahhabi Islam has been exported in sufficient measure to determine the nature of jihad there. That the reverse might be true, with Arab fighters and financiers importing the jihad from these regions to the Middle East, is not seriously considered, although it is certainly true of Al-Qaeda and the phenomenon of the so called Arab-Afghans - militants who returned after the anti-Soviet war in Afghanistan to their homes in the Middle East and founded new jihad movements there.

In general the importance of non-Arab Muslims and of non-Arab Islam to the Middle East has been underestimated, as borne out by the example of Iraq in early 2005: Ayatollah Sistani was that country's great Shiite authority, even though he is an Iranian whose Arabic remains heavily accented by his native Farsi. Much of Sistani's authority in Iraq, moreover, derives from his control and disbursement of funds raised by Shia populations elsewhere, a very significant portion of which comes from India and Pakistan. Sistani's constituency in the subcontinent, then, through his agent in Mumbai, might well hold a key to the Ayatollah's importance in Iraq.

This Shiite example apart, the presence of large non-Arab working populations in the Arabian Peninsula, as well as the dominance of non-Arab Muslims in the formulation and dissemination of Islamic ideas globally, especially in languages like English, renders nonsensical any notion that the Arab Middle East is the original homeland of radical Islam. The Taliban provides a perfect illustration of the kind of movement that has repeatedly been described as a foreign import. It was supposedly influenced by Deobandi practices from India, themselves funded and influenced by Saudi Wahhabism, and by Wahhabi practices coming directly from Saudi Arabia - both of which were imparted in Pakistani seminaries, and were supposedly legalistic and scripturalist in the extreme. And yet the Taliban leader Mullah Omar chose in Kandahar to drape himself in a mantle belonging to the Prophet and declare himself the Commander of the Faithful, a title used for the caliphs who were meant to be Muhammad's successors - he was in fact flatteringly called a caliph by no less a person than Osama bin Laden. In what way could this coronation be understood as conforming to any Deobandi or Wahhabi teaching? If anything the vision of Mullah Omar donning the Prophet's

'a global movement like the jihad depends upon the erosion of traditional religious and political allegiances for its very existence'

mantle suggests Sufi and especially Shia themes, since the latter believe in the apostolic succession of those members of Muhammad's family whom he famously covered with his cloak. And it is precisely such charismatic forms of authority that both the Deobandis and Wahhabis are supposed to execrate.

There is nothing more calculated to degrade the celebrated scripturalist or legalist forms of Islam associated with these groups, tied as they are to the authority of a class of scholarly commentators, than the institution of a self-proclaimed Commander of the Faithful - one who claimed, in addition, to have received divine instruction in his dreams. By acts such as these, the Taliban not only assumed an immediate superiority over their Saudi or Pakistani teachers; they also forced from the latter an acknowledgement of religious forms and practices that were barely dreamt of in the Deobandi and Wahhabi schools. Suddenly it seemed as if the direction of Islamic influence had been reversed, with teachers in the centre taking dictation from students on the periphery.

Is a genealogical mode of explanation at all credible in a situation where participants in the jihad come from all manner of national and religious backgrounds? Quite apart from the hijackers in New York or the bombers in Madrid who betrayed no obvious signs of Muslim piety, we know that in places like Afghanistan, too, fighters came from many different and even opposed Islamic affiliations, which are generally kept far apart by scholarly genealogists. But the plethora of groups, often very exclusive, participating in the jihad does not indicate their alliance for some common cause. It may however signal the fact that a global movement like the jihad depends upon the erosion of traditional religious and political allegiances for its very existence. After all Al-Qaeda, like other global movements, possesses an extraordinarily diverse membership, one that is not united by way of any cultic or ideological commonality, to say nothing about any common class, ethnic or personal background. Indeed it can only function as the network it is by disrupting and disregarding old-fashioned forms of political and religious allegiance.

If there exists any genealogy within which Al-Qaeda can be located, it is a mystical or heretical one. For example there is a widespread rejection by the jihad of the classical doctrine of holy war as a collective or political obligation similar to that of choosing a ruler or administering justice. One implication of treating holy war as an individual ethical obligation like prayer is that it becomes spiritualised and finally puts the jihad beyond the pragmatism of political life. So whereas liberal as well as fundamentalist Muslims tried to instrumentalise Islam by attributing social, political or economic functions to its beliefs or practices, the jihad does just the opposite - its task is to de-instrumentalise Islam and make it part of everyday ethics.

There is a tradition of holy war that does exactly this, one that possesses all the requisite ingredients of religious fervour and popular support, and has, in addition, nothing to do with the juridical politics of a state. Such a tradition of jihad, while it might well have given rise to states, was characteristic of charismatic, mystical and heretical movements, often messianic in nature, that were located at the peripheries of Islamic power or authority, and frequently directed against them as much as against any infidel presence. Indeed all the great jihad movements from the eighteenth to the twentieth centuries were Sufi ones. It is hardly accidental, therefore, that by far the most popular examples of the ghazi or holy warrior in the Muslim world happen to be members of Sufi or mystic fraternities, whose tombs continue to be places of pilgrimage, healing and spiritual succour.

In many ways today's jihad builds upon these Sufi ventures. It, too, is located on the peripheries of the Muslim world, geographically, politically and religiously; it operates now in places like Chechnya, Afghanistan, Pakistan and India, as well as in Thailand and the Philippines. Like its predecessors, the jihad in our times is also peripheral as a set of practices, being charismatic, heretical and even mystical. And like these holy wars of the past, the jihad, too, attempts to move such populist and non-juridical elements to the centre of the Islamic world as part of its struggle. Yet Al-Qaeda's jihad does not replace one sort of authority by another, for instance Salafism by Sufism, but fragments Muslim forms of authority altogether, thus democratising Islam itself. What emerges from this fragmentation is a new kind of individual, or rather a new form of Muslim individualism.

The global landscape of Al-Qaeda

The new Muslim individual brought into being by Al-Qaeda's jihad moves across a different kind of landscape than that with which scholars tend to be familiar. Let us look at how that prime location of Muslim radicalism, the Middle East, constitutes such a landscape for this individual. The Middle East today is a truly dispersed entity, with much of its press headquartered in London, its language used by Arab and non-Arab alike, and even its jihad originating elsewhere. Indeed the Middle East might well be grounded in a specific territory only by its oil wells. But even this definition disintegrates on closer inspection. The oil-rich kingdoms of the Persian Gulf, for example, which play such a large role in the jihad, from providing it with funds to supplying homes and constituencies, were initially created, governed and exploited by British imperialism in the form of the Government of India. It was this government and its Indian subjects that founded, managed and manned the oil industries of these countries, including Iraq, till well after the end of British rule in 1947.

Even today this area is linked demographically, economically and culturally more to the Indian Subcontinent, South-East Asia and East Africa than it is to the rest of the Middle East. So apart from the large foreign populations settled in these monarchies, sometimes forming the majority of their inhabitants, many of the historical centres in this extended region owe their existence to commercial links with Asia and Africa. Aden, for instance, from whence Osama bin Laden's family originated (his father leaving this declining city for new opportunities in Saudi Arabia), was an important place in its time only because it served as a link in the British route to and from India; and it also possessed, therefore, a large Indian population. Aden, indeed, was in some ways the Dubai of its time - a cosmopolitan city more similar in every way to Bombay or London than to the Yemeni capital of Sana. This is why the common description of the Bin Laden family as Yemeni is as much correct as it is not.

But the relationship between the Persian Gulf and points south or east of it is not all one-way. Just to take the example of India: this small region provides that huge country with the bulk of its foreign investment, mostly in the form of remittances from Indians settled there; it keeps its national airline financially viable by ferrying Indians to and from various sheikhdoms; and it acts as a major centre both for its entertainment industry and crime syndicates. Given all this, it should come as no surprise that a Christian migrant from the Indian state of Kerala could be far more integrated and at home in a place like Dubai than an Arabic-speaking Muslim migrant from Morocco. After all, one is as likely to encounter Urdu or Swahili in public places here as to encounter Arabic.

Most important in its fragmentation as a Middle Eastern region, however, is the fact that the Persian Gulf's disparate populations are not linked by any relations, whether social, political or economic, that happen to be based on citizenship. Foreigners in the Gulf tend to have no rights of permanent residence, let alone equal rights with those defined as indigenes - who themselves are by no means equal citizens of nation states. All relations among these populations therefore tend to be cosmopolitan instead of national. The moment that citizenship rights are denied to a segment of a state's population, especially an enormous population such as that of foreigners in the Gulf, citizenship itself disappears as an aspect of national uniformity, along with many other notions of a common culture and solidarity. The end result is perhaps a kind of market managed by rules that have nothing to do with political representation or participation as we recognise them.

The global marketplace: home of the jihad

This curious world, which may function in various forms within immigrant and other cosmopolitan enclaves elsewhere, seems to mirror rather closely the world of the jihad itself. It is, after all, the world of the global marketplace, and it includes within its ambit not only multinational corporations or transnational trading networks, but also the international students, economic migrants, illegal aliens and political refugees who form part and parcel of these commercial enterprises. And we know that the global transactions of the jihad, along with its incredibly mobile operators, use and indeed emerge from such networks and enclaves, in which an old-fashioned politics of intentionality and collective mobilisation, based on some common need, interest or idea, has been ruled out.

One has only to consider the remarkable peregrinations of the 9/11 hijackers - which ran the gamut from German universities and Afghan training camps to American flight schools, passing through the immigrant enclaves of European cities in the process - to realise that such networks and enclaves operate according to the norms of the global marketplace. And this is regardless of whether or not they happen to be located in traditional nation states where political and other relations are meant to be defined in the language of citizenship. All of this makes for a whole new world of cosmopolitan relations between people.

I want to end this essay by returning to its beginning, more precisely to my claim that the global arena does not yet possess a political form proper to itself. Al-Qaeda's actions and rhetoric continuously invoke the spectre of a global community that has as yet no formal existence of its own. And this is what allows its jihad to draw upon the forms and even the vocabulary of other global movements such as environmental and pacifist ones, all of which bear a family resemblance to one another.

What Al-Qaeda does is to invoke the spectre of a global community, not by providing an alternative to liberal democracy, but rather by universalising - albeit in its own particular way - its ideals. Earlier movements of resistance or terror had advanced critiques of existing

Al-Qaeda, spectre of globalisation

conditions, for instance of capitalism or imperialism, and offered alternatives to them. This was the case with Marxists and Anarchists as well as with nationalists and fundamentalists. But, like the more pacific global movements that are its peers, Al-Qaeda's jihad poses no real criticism of existing conditions and possesses no alternative to take their place.

Osama bin Laden's rhetoric has consistently voiced a desire for global equality between the Islamic world and the West. Having accused America of hypocrisy as far as its advancement of this equality is concerned, Bin Laden turns his attention to the only form in which such equality is possible: the equality of death. This is why he has repeatedly emphasised the need for an equivalence of terror between the Muslim world and America, as if this were the only form in which the two might come together and even communicate one with the other. For Al-Qaeda terror is the only form in which global equality is now available. It therefore functions as the dark side of America's own democracy, as inseparable from it as its evil twin.

International and interdisciplinary conference
Countering consumerism: religious and secular responses

 ISET

20 - 22 April 2006
Graduate centre
London Metropolitan University

 LONDON metropolitan university

An interdisciplinary conference linking the themes of 'Spirituality' and 'Consumerism'

The Conference will provide an opportunity to review ideas about the 'good life' and to explore both the common ground and the sites of tension between secular and religious responses to contemporary consumer culture. Speakers include: Jackie Ashley, Zygmunt Bauman (tbc), Colin Campbell, Tim Cooper, Rt Revd Graham Cray, Peter Harvey, Jean Lambert MEP, Ziauddin Sardar, Kate Soper, Elizabeth Wilson.

The conference is organised by the ESRC/AHRC Cultures of Consumption Phase Two research project on 'Alternative Hedonism and the Theory and Politics of Consumption'

 Arts & Humanities Research Council

For more information about this conference and details of how to register please go to: www.londonmet.ac.uk/iset/conf

 E·S·R·C ECONOMIC & SOCIAL RESEARCH COUNCIL

Rehabilitating pacification

Then and now, Iraq and Vietnam

Kurt Jacobsen

Kurt Jacobsen *shows how pacification has been rehabilitated as a viable strategy for the US military.*

'We are not into nation-building. And we're not into nation-building because of the way our military has to operate'. Senator John Murtha, in his outspoken criticism of the Iraq war in November 2005, quoted this statement by President Bush, made when he ran for office in 2000. As Senator Murtha went on to point out, the logic of the American military meant that 'We've got to go in and level the place, destroy a place'. Yet, as he also argued, 'when we destroy a place, we lose the very thing that's absolutely essential to winning the insurgency'.

Murtha here exposes the contradictions of 'pacification' - a policy that was a key part of the US armoury in the Vietnam war. Pacification was responsible for the killing of hundreds of thousands of civilians as well as combatants, and it was, of course, entirely unsuccessful. For Vietnam era beholders especially, the term is simply a euphemism for vicious military suppression of popular resistance during interventions abroad. Yet, as this article documents, this is the strategy that is currently being rehabilitated and brought back into service as the war in Iraq continues.

According to the OED, 'pacification' denotes 'the condition of being pacified, appeasement, conciliation'. A helpful example given is an 'ordinance or decree enacted by a prince or state to put an end to strife or discontent'. The verb 'to pacify' means 'to allay the anger, excitement, or agitation (of a person); to calm; quiet; to appease', but more ominously its meaning also includes 'to reduce to peaceful submission', as when Hobbes writes: 'Counts … were left to govern and defend places conquered and pacified'. Who today fails to recognise the rueful ancient quotation regarding Roman retributive techniques: 'they make a desert and call it peace'?

The term pacification, in its contemporary use, has been around as long as the ugly services it comprises have been required by irked occupiers. In its contemporary usage it could be read as including the meanings both of appeasement and coercion, carrot and stick. This is useful for those proposing it as a strategy. And any useful procedure in a governing elite's repertoire is bound to make a strong comeback when events seem to require it, even if it may take on a new, PR-prompted, verbal guise. So, one US government response to reverses in Iraq has been to resurrect the counterinsurgency programmes of yesteryear. These have been duly reinterpreted by right-wing scholars as a parade of proud successes - even including the military fiasco that was Vietnam. According to these starry-eyed analysts, counterinsurgency, suitably refined, will suppress crazed Iraqi resistance. Accordingly, as early as 2004, some $3 billion of the Iraq appropriation budget in the US was already slated for covert military and paramilitary operations. And you don't need a military genius to tell you that these operations will target not only armed Iraqi 'rebels' - as the Pentagon calls them - but also any nationalist opponent of the US occupation, including nonviolent ones.

Counterinsurgency operations in the 1960s referred to such programmes as civic action and pacification, and these can be loosely defined as the employment of military resources for purposes other than conventional warfare. An infamous example of this was the Phoenix programme in Vietnam, which was designed to 'neutralise' (through assassination, kidnapping and torture) South Vietnamese civilian resistance. One manically optimistic take on the failures of such a strategy in Vietnam was that the Marines (or CIA or Army special forces, in different takes) had acquired a counterinsurgency stock of wisdom built over time but that it had not been wisely tapped and brought to bear as it ought to have been in Vietnam.[1] Here is an impregnable belief that violent techniques will work, regardless of the local context, or of the parameters imposed by the reigning political coalition.

As former CIA counter-terrorism chief Robert Dreyfuss recently observed of Iraq (*American Prospect*, January 2004), 'They're clearly cooking up joint teams to do Phoenix-like things, like they did in Vietnam'. The aim is to create an indigenous security force that will carry out counter-insurgency tactics against local resistance. The CIA presence in Iraq is augmented by elite military units such as Delta Force and the Navy SEALs, whose ultimate objective is to establish an Iraqi security force loyal to the US. Local militiamen have mostly been drawn from Iraqi exile groups who have plenty of long-nursed grudges to settle, but US forces have not been too proud or bashful to work with select former members of Saddam Hussein's secret police. Under Defence Secretary Rumsfeld, secret commando units were given a free hand globally to strike at suspected terrorists, even though authorities admit that poor intelligence often results in the wrong victims being fingered. Apparently, such small mishaps hardly count, even as 'collateral damage'. The local people are not supposed to mind.

It's an old, gory story. Iconic images of Yank soldiers burning Vietnamese villages hark back to the systematic atrocities of American forces in the Philippines in 1898-1901, and then further back to the long campaigns through which the gallant US military swept much of the North American continent clean of meddlesome natives. Pacification has always needed a potent domestic propaganda component: states depend on their power to define the situations they get into. No one knows how well this 'power to define' worked better than children who grew up playing cowboys and Indians in the celebratory post-war John Wayne movie era: the innately backward natives had their merits, too bad they got in the way of manifest destiny.

Go far enough West and you wind up in the East, and exploits here are a bit harder to explain away to a populace taught to hate imperialism (or at least the epicene European kind). In South East Asia the Americans failed spectacularly to make their definitions, or their dominance, stick. But now they are attempting

---

1. See, for example, Larry Cable, who posits that the lessons the Marine Corps learned from earlier pacification interventions were not properly institutionalised and diffused, in *Conflict of Myths: The Development of American Counterinsurgency Doctrine in the Vietnam War*, New York University Press 1986, p96.

a similar feat in Iraq and Afghanistan. In the first year of the insurgency after the Iraq invasion it was deemed the height of sophistication for critics to dismiss Vietnam analogies as alarmist, puerile and overdrawn. But by the end of 2005 even the most pedigreed and housebroken of pundits were not so sure any more. Still, the propaganda war never ends. Many of Bush's aides today buy into the belief that pacification in Vietnam worked, so why not try it again.

Rehabilitating Vietnam strategy

The revisionist battles over Vietnam since 1975 hinge on the resuscitated view that counter-insurgency tactics succeeded. And they succeeded, proponents cheerily assert, with the most terrible irony - in that their success came at the very moment a supposedly needless American withdrawal got under way.[2] 'We' won, but foolishly bugged out. The implication is that the strategy was sound all along, and only required a little more time for the necessary fine-tuning to kick in to create a happy little neo-colony.

The widespread 'we won even though we scarpered' interpretation sprang up the instant the 1973 peace accords were signed, got great play among military buffs, and then resurged unrepentantly into public view in the early 1990s, with a further revival as Bush II took office. The stupendously strained assumption is that there was a way to win the war without annihilating the bulk of the population, going nuclear, or expanding the conflict into China.

To take one example: Mark Moyar's imaginative account of the Phoenix assassination programme, a book embraced by some military men (and scholarly wannabees), is laced with jaw-dropping implausibilities, contradictions and tendentious argument.[3] The study is a sublime outcome of the Abu Ghraib

---

2. See Fox Butterfield, 'The New Vietnam Scholarship', *The New York Times Magazine*, 13.2.83; Robert Manning, 'We Could Have Won Vietnam', *New York Times*, 12.11.89; Angelo Codevilla, 'The Bureaucrat & the War', *Commentary*, January 1990; and Harry G. Summers, Jr., 'Vietnam Reconsidered', *The New Republic* (12.7.82). Pro-war Vietnam books include Guenther Lewy, *America In Vietnam* (1978); Harry Summers, *On Strategy: A Critical Analysis of the Vietnam War* (1982); Hosmer, Kellner and Jenkins, *The Fall of South Vietnam* (1986); Scott Thompson and Donaldson Frizzell (eds), *The Lessons of Vietnam* (1977); and William E. Colby with James McCarger, *Lost Victory: A Firsthand Account of America's Sixteen-Year Involvement in Vietnam* (1989).
3. Marx Moyar, *Phoenix and the Birds of Prey: The CIA's Secret Campaign to Destroy the Viet Cong*, Naval Institute Press 1997. For a different view see Douglas Valentine, *The Phoenix Program: A Shattering Account of the Most Ambitious and Closely-Guarded Operation of the Vietnam War*, Morrow 1990.

methodological approach to history: torture the data until it yields exactly what the author wants to see. Mass murder can become 'an effective counterinsurgency tool' - even if you murder uninvolved people. According to Moyar, the locals will understand if well-meaning authorities snuff the wrong person every now and then, if it's all in a good cause. The fact that so shoddy a book can be seized on as 'balanced' and as bona fide evidence even in some academic circles is a rather disturbing sign.

The Phoenix programme was designed to help the US military attain a gruesome 'crossover point', where dead and wounded exceeded the National Liberation Front's (NLF) ability to replenish recruits. During Nixon's first two and a half years, the State Department admitted that the CIA-run Programme murdered or abducted 35,708 Vietnamese civilians. Ex-Phoenix operatives in this 'anything goes' programme revealed that sometimes orders were given to kill South Vietnamese Army and even US military personnel who were considered security risks.[4] Phoenix was not calculated to court hearts and minds - except insofar as 'black teams' would go out, usually dressed in enemy gear, with the ensuing assassinations then blamed on the NLF.[5]

Another rehabilitator of pacification is Zalin Grant, whose book *Facing the Phoenix*, the publisher's blurb tells us, is based on the reckonings of a South Vietnamese spy, whose plan to defeat communists by community action 'was perverted by the CIA'. According to NameBase, a rightwing website, Grant believes that: 'certain players had a good handle on how to neutralize the enemy through local political action and enlightened aid programs. Just as they were making significant progress, however, they were defeated by corruption in Saigon and by big-bang, big-bucks conventional-warfare mongers like William Westmoreland'.[6] So, if only you had disposed of the regime you were defending, and the US military authorities who were defending it, you would have won. This reverie constitutes perfectly logical thinking in some circles. Another study attests that prudent Americans, through the sagacious Land-to-the-Tiller reforms, had won over most

---

4. Covert Action Information Bulletin (now Covert Action Quarterly) Summer 1982, p52.
5. Brian Toohey and William Pinwell, *Oyster: The Story of the Australian Secret Intelligence Service*, Heinemann, Victoria 1989, pp87-88.
6. Zalin Grant, *Facing the Phoenix: The CIA and the Political Defeat of the United States in Vietnam*, Norton 1991.

Vietnamese villagers by 1970 - villagers who good-naturedly forgave the Americans for innumerable mishaps, 'relocations', rough handlings, and collateral damage because they knew the nice Yanks were only protecting them and meant well. A 'can-do' spirit doubtless has its place in the military, but in scholarship and intelligence analysis it is a source of rampant distortion. But Bush's White House established an Office of Special Plans, and other disinformation units, to create just such rampant self-serving distortions in intelligence data, in order to mislead Congress and the public.

If the President or the CIA director tells you, as a direct employee, what you must find, what else can you do (except whistleblow and/or resign)? Why, however, do scholars buckle to official views? Well, for one thing, there is always remunerative work for skilful people willing to tell hard-line bosses what they want to hear. A suffocatingly managerial mentality can then come into play among ambitious scholars, who accept as their own the edicts of their nation's policy elites, yet thereafter sincerely assume that they are merely performing purely scientific tasks. One orthodox international relations studies axiom, for example, is that where mindless (always mindless) resistance arises, more than proportionate force must be deployed. And force must be seen to work, even if it really doesn't. Once these edicts are accepted, the task is to work out how to carry them out, not to question the underlying assumptions.

This was precisely the conformist mindset attributed by Noam Chomsky to the New Mandarins of the Vietnam era: devout, cold-blooded, hard-nosed, numerical and officious.[7] They were then, and are today, ready to comply with incessant urging from the top to convert 'a pleasing hypothesis into a fact' - which, as Hannah Arendt reminds us, is a highly fecund source of official lies.[8]

For example, in the face of any revelation of systematic murder and intimidation campaigns by authorities in Vietnam, the right-wing answer always is that they (the NLF/NVA) did it too - they manage to ignore that they didn't do it a level anywhere near the US/South Vietnamese scale, and that they didn't do it to Americans who managed to stay in Detroit or Miami or LA. Lately, these rehabilitative studies have become grist to the mill for

7. Noam Chomsky, *American Power and the New Mandarins*, Pantheon, 1968.
8. Hannah Arendt, *Crises of the Republic*, Harcourt, Brace, Jovanovich, 1972, p42.

the purveyors of rational choice analyses - a direct heir to 1960s era systems analysis. The soft issue of social justice (because it is not measurable) cannot arise within the conceptual boundaries of rational choice theory, and therefore it does not matter.[9]

The case for counterinsurgency and land reform relies on warmed-over data, such as the US Hamlet Evaluation Survey, conducted by government agents in 1970-71 and re-evaluated recently in a massive study by David Elliot, formerly of the far from impeccable Rand Corporation.[10] The extremely dicey fact that these evaluations rely on agencies ultimately catering to counterinsurgency objectives - and that information was extracted under conditions of duress - either does not register, or else is acknowledged and then never mentioned again as the analysis proceeds. Hence, in the twenty-first century one can look back and draw again on the evidence that led to the conclusion that 'every quantitative measure we have indicates that we are winning this war' (as systems analyst fanatic and Defence Secretary Robert McNamara indeed said in October 1962), to see that we should indeed have won it. According to Lewis Lapham, McNamara himself was 'was caught up in a dream of power that substituted the databases of a preferred fiction for the texts of common fact … What was real was the image of war that appeared on the flowcharts and computer screens. What was not real was the presence of pain, suffering, mutilation, and death'.[11] McNamara since has done an (imperfect) penance. But fresh and unchastened McNamara mentalities continue to proliferate.[12]

Hearts and hectares

One of the main myths resuscitated by the current round of Vietnam revisionism is that the 'land to the tiller' programme of 1970 was winning hearts and minds in great numbers in the early 1970s. This ignores three things: firstly, by 1970 great swathes of South Vietnam were already largely under NLF control;

---

9. See Stathis N. Kalyvas and Matthew Kocher, 'Violence and Control in Civil War: An Analysis of the Hamlet Evaluation Study', paper given at University of Chicago, 2003.
10. David Elliot, *The Vietnamese War: Revolution and Social Change in the Mekong Delta, 1930-1978*, M. E. Sharpe 2003.
11. Lewis Lapham, *Waiting for the Barbarians*, Verso 1997, p30.
12. See *Fog of War* and my review of it in *New Politics*, Summer 2004. See also Michael Rustin's piece in this issue.

secondly, in these areas land had already been widely redistributed; and thirdly, the Thieu reforms were not very redistributive and not very popular. The US administration believed the 'land to the tiller' programme built on previous 'land reforms' by the Southern regime, but the record belies this claim. By the 1950s, 80 per cent of peasants living in the Mekong Delta were tenants: just 1 per cent of the populace owned 44 per cent of rice land in South Vietnam overall. The land 'reforms' of the Diem government had actually restored to landlords land previously redistributed by the Vietn Minh before partition. In NLF strongholds in South Vietnam, by contrast, land was redistributed to peasants by the insurgents; for example, by 1960 the NLF had redistributed 77 per cent of arable land in the My Tho province Elliot studied. (The first visitor after American forces had secured a village, typically, would be the absentee landlord coming to collect back rent.) The 'land to the tiller' programme in actuality featured a Stolypin-like emphasis on creating a class of rich peasants. For example, the sanctioned distribution of uncultivated land in insecure areas (full of unexploded ordnance and trigger-happy patrols) required capital if the land was to be put to use, for which only usurious loans were available.[13] The weak measures of the Thieu reforms could not compete with the real redistribution organised by the insurgents.

Elliot says the land to the tiller programme made no impact because land already had been redistributed, mostly by the enemy the government was fighting. The pacified areas were in fact largely 'nod and wink' arrangements, in that they were used by communist cadres for what amounted to R & R. 'What the Pentagon describes as "secure areas" in Vietnam', Kolko observed, 'is often a staging and economic base as secure and vital to the NLF as its explicitly identified liberated zones.' If the NLF had not been so well entrenched, where would their offensives have sprung from? At all points the South Vietnamese Government (GVN) was shot through with NLF and NVA spies and informers.

Yet punctilious US monitors claimed that US/GVN forces controlled 67 per cent of the South Vietnam population on the eve of the 1968 Tet Offensive.[14] The same sources imperturbably claim that US/GVN control soared

---

13. Ngo Vinh Long, 'Land Reform.' *Bulletin of Concerned Asian Scholars*, February 1971, p50.
14. Gabriel Kolko, 'The Political Significance of the Center for Vietnamese Studies and Programs', *Bulletin of Concerned Asian Scholars* Feb 1971, p42. Also see Kolko's *Vietnam: Anatomy of a War*, Allen & Unwin 1986.

even higher afterward. On what basis could one credit either claim? The reports the pacification enthusiasts rely upon are equivocal at best, and, often enough, contradictory. Elliot found that the Mekong Delta area was 'strongly pro-VC' in 1969-70, well after the fighting during the Tet offensive had supposedly killed off the majority of guerrilla insurgents, not to mention innumerable Phoenix forays and 9th Infantry division sweeps. Elliot also found that few locals 'defected from the war effort'. Studies by Eric Bergerud, James Trullinger, Jeffrey Pace and Jayne Werner and David Hunt likewise testify that the districts they studied were overwhelmingly in favour of the NLF in 1964-65 when the US ground troop escalation began, and remained so throughout.[15]

W hat was supposed to have changed such that the attitudes of villagers became favourable (rather than outwardly acquiescent) towards the US/GVN forces? The customary case made is that, after many corruption-driven fits and starts, land reform did occur and that, once property was handed over, the peasants transformed into 'middle peasants' and heart-warmingly market-oriented individualists (as Irish peasants had done under less combative conditions in the very early twentieth century). We have to ask, however, whether the analysts are forcing the data to fit their framework. Those few land reform specialists not linked to the Southern authorities found only 'a class-oriented program' ... 'no amount of wishful or ideological thinking could turn Diem, Kah, Ky or Thieu into champions of the laboring poor'.[16] The hope was, according to a highly subjective definition, that one and a half hectares of land would be enough to make a loyal 'middle' peasant out of a tenant. However, the evidence seems to indicate that middle peasants were more likely to produce NLF recruits, since they had the resources and ability to participate. There was no steady erosion in communist or community ties on the part of the wealthier peasants.

Any imputed gains were illusory or else temporary. Underlying grievances were never meant to be addressed. But the census-taking attitude meant that

---

15. Eric Bergerud, *Dynamics of Defeat*; James Trullinger, *Village at War*, Longman, 1980; Jeffrey Race, *War Comes to Long An*, University of California 1972; David Hunt and Jayne Werner, *The American War in Vietnam*, Cornell University Press 1993; and Ngo Vinh Long, *Before The Revolution*, MIT Press 1973.

16. Robert K Brigham and Martin J, Murray, 'Conflicting Interpretations of the Vietnam war', in *Bulletin of Concerned Asian Scholars* 26, 1-2 (January-June 1994), p. 117. Also see Marylin Young, *The Vietnam Wars*, Harper 1991.

opinions were taken at face value. Ngo Vinh Long points out that, for people under a repressive regime and foreign occupation, the questions, 'Do you believe the people should be masters' and 'Do you believe in democracy' were understood as being more resonant of the NLF and the North than Saigon, but were coded to favour the latter (for reference see note 13). So far as the Southern insurgency was concerned, as even a US Major General (William DuPuy) acknowledged, 'when NLF casualties got too high ... they just backed off and waited'.[17] The NLF held the initiative at all times, including the initiative to taper off when tactical exigencies warranted.

After Tet

Tet itself, according to Elliot, was as much a popular uprising as anything else; David Hunt calls it 'the greatest of the peasant revolts'. There are, however, some who attempt to argue that Tet was a victory for the US/GVN. One unchallenged cliché, for example, is that Tet was a political victory but a military defeat. But this is a short-sighted and ultimately unimportant distinction. The insurgent forces sustained very heavy losses but this did not lead to any wavering in support on the part of survivors. The US high command view was that the countryside was regained by revolutionaries as troops diverted into the cities to drive out the NLF. They acknowledged that the enemy still to a large extent controlled the countryside.[18] Furthermore, the customary figures don't weigh the NLF losses against the two hundred thousand released prisoners in all the cities and jails who refilled the ranks.[19] It remained possible for the NLF and NVA to continue to be able to launch equally devastating offensives after Tet, and Generals Westmoreland and Wheeler both privately acknowledged that Tet was no victory.

Hunt found that, contrary to pacification lore, 'US/GVN sweeps and mass killings seem to have pushed fence-sitters over the edge', so that many volunteered for the NLF. Blaufarb argues that the crime of Phoenix was 'ineffectiveness, indiscriminateness, and, in some areas at least, the violation

---

17. Robert D. Schulzinger, *A Time for War: The US and Vietnam*, Oxford University Press 1997, p200.
18. *Pentagon Papers*, Defence Department 1971.
19. Bruce Franklin, *Vietnam and Other American Fantasies*, University of Massachusetts 2000, p95.

of the local norms to the extent that it appeared to the villagers to be a threat to them in the peaceful performance of their daily business'. His view is that the Americans involved 'erred in not appreciating the extent to which the pathology of Vietnamese society would distort an apparently sound concept'.[20]

The unadorned objective in My Tho province was 'to destroy rather than "pacify" the rural communities'. The bombing, pillaging, refugee flight, the GVN and NLF drafts, cadres killed, and cumulative hardships all led to a retreat. Even so, the six villages of one official Hamlet Evaluation Study remained 'nearly completely controlled by the revolution as much in January 1968 as a year before'. This unexpected result, for certain analysts, can be comprehended only in the terms of a game of rival gang warfare. There is no room for the ideas of nationalism or solidarity, only for self-regarding groups who compel obedience; this, though, cannot explain why the NLF were vastly more successful than the US/GVN, despite taking unbelievable punishment. For if rational choice were the NLF's operating code, the war would have been over in quick order.

Pacification was a flop from the start. Carrot and stick, at the first sign of sustained resistance, becomes all stick. Disembedded press members, such as David Halberstam and Peter Arnett, saw the Strategic Hamlet Programme disintegrating before their very eyes as early as 1965, despite happy talk reports to the contrary.[21] But the tradition of 'doctoring' reports goes back at least as far as the RAF 'revision' of its use of phosphorous bombs, chemical weapons and gas upon villages in the Middle East in the 1920s, stretching through the Nixon administration's secret bombing of Cambodia and Laos to initial denials of use of phosphorous bombs in Iraq today. As Henry Cabot Lodge told McNamara: 'If you think these people are going to tell you or say in front of [General] Harkin what they really think unless it is what Harkin thinks, you just don't know the army' (Prochnau, p438).

In the 1960s and early 1970s, government agencies were divided in their views on the effectiveness of pacification, depending to a large extent on whether or not they understood the Vietnamese conception of protracted war.

---

20. Douglas S. Blaufarb, *The Counterinsurgency Era: U.S. Doctrine and Performance, 1950 to the Present*, Free Press 1977, p276.
21. William Prochnau, *Once Upon a Distant War*, Vintage 1996, p 419.

Chalmers Johnson told an interviewer later that: 'many senior analysts were passionately opposed to President Johnson and Richard Nixon's policies, and after the Pentagon Papers had been made public many of the analysts were quietly exultant that their pessimistic estimates of whether the US could win the war were now in an official part of the public record.'[22]

And in spite of all the work to revise the history of pacification, it is clear, as Senator John Murtha's recent controversial speeches indicate, that the Pentagon today is also pessimistic - or at least seriously divided - about the prospects for pacification in Iraq. Even without a leak of Pentagon Papers proportions, rationales for the Iraq intervention are unravelling.

Conclusion

Could the sorely expensive Iraqi occupation, under any imaginable circumstances, have succeeded? The quaint delusion is widespread, even among liberal pundits, that Bush might have avoided an intractable insurgency if only he had made a shrewder move here or there. Maybe if the Army had been kept intact, things would have worked out. Maybe if Saddam loyalists had been kept behind their desks, things would have worked out. Maybe if the impulsive US had waited to amass a military force twice its size (as many Military commanders urged) before invading, things would have worked. Maybe if honest contractors had gotten electricity and water running again, things would have worked out. Maybe if the US rulers wouldn't privatise everything in sight to sell it off to cronies, things would work out.

So goes the mournful litany - with verses added almost daily. Presumably, then, if all the conditions above were met, Iraqis of all stripes would sit perfectly still with hands folded while the West siphoned away their resources. (The British military's conceit that they possessed a magic formula for conducting a 'decent' occupation finally has also crumbled under scrutiny.[23]) Farfetched scenarios indeed. As Glenn Perusek has shown, the Coalition Provisional Authority has established a parallel government structure of Commissioners and inspectors-general, who, elections notwithstanding, will

---

22. Chalmers Johnson, 'The CIA and Me,' *Bulletin of Concerned Asian Scholars* 29, 1 (Jan-March 1997), p36.
23. Robert Fisk, 'Turning a Blind Eye to Murder and Abuse in Basra,' *Counterpunch/The Independent* 24/25 September 2005.

control Iraq's chief ministries for the next five years. As he argues, they mean to stick around, no matter what.[24] Yes, one might concede that it all might have worked out if a US government of a radically different character had invaded - except that such a government would have read intelligence data honestly and therefore opted not to invade.

Given the running sore of Iraq, the highly apparent duplicity at the top, the growing uproar over leaks and corruption, and a sluggish economy, Bush's supreme problem now seems likely to be how to 'pacify' his own restive citizenry.

---

24. Glenn Perusek, 'The US Occupation and Resistance in Iraq', *New Politics*, winter 2005.

Afghanistan and the failures of secular modernisation

Soon after Kamal Ataturk introduced secular laws, education and constitution for the new republic of Turkey in the early 1920s, King Khan in Afghanistan enthusiastically tried to imitate the Turkish example. But he moved so rashly that his efforts to emancipate Afghan women and to modernise society stirred up more resistance that his regime could overcome. Amanullah had taken over the throne in Kabul when his father Amir Habibullah was assassinated in 1919, though he was not the oldest son. His father had played a clever conciliatory role as a buffer between the British and Russians, but his son, who was not well disposed towards British India, soon went to war with the British, a conflict that proved inconclusive. The British, unable to conquer him, then started courting him. Amanullah became the first Afghan ruler to visit Europe. There he was feted and entertained by European powers, who competed to gain his favour in order to wield influence over the politics in the region.

The British were the superpower on the Eastern border so he grudgingly dealt with them. In London he was treated to a regal reception. His half-Syrian wife queen Soraya, however, was photographed partying in western dress - scandalous images, which were duly distributed throughout Afghanistan. These shocking photos were more than enough to enrage the conservative Afghan chiefs. There is good reason, though not solid proof, to believe that British intelligence was behind the impressively efficient distribution of these upsetting photos. Whatever the case, the photos were symbolic of the clash between the modernising king and the conservative religious establishment. On his return from abroad the King, unashamed, promptly ordered his subjects to don western clothes, including shoes with laces, an oddity to which they were not accustomed. Mullahs countered by issuing fatwas against the King, declaring him an infidel.

In the event, Amanullah's attempts to introduce secular governance to Afghanistan failed. During these large-scale social experiments his key adviser had been Sir Francis Humphrey, head of the British legation in Kabul, and it was Sir Francis who eventually arranged the king's exile when he was deposed by Baccha Saqqa. Baccha Saqqa was a nondescript hoodlum, who ransacked Kabul in 1929 and started massacring every loyal follower of the king that he could find. He became for a short time the ruler of Afghanistan, though he seemed to have emerged from virtually nowhere. This was largely because the Mullahs, who had been deprived of their cherished social status by the king, found him a very handy tool for the restoration of their own authority. Sir Francis (nimble diplomat or successful plotter) immediately got on good terms with the usurper of the throne, but after a few months Nadir Khan, a former minister of Amanullah, deposed and hanged him. Nadir Khan then succeeded to leadership but he was careful not to disturb the religious groups who had dominated Afghan society before King Amanullah's thwarted reforms. As king, Nadir Khan (who became then Nadir Shah) was able to stabilise the monarchy, though he too was assassinated in 1933. The monarchy continued unmolested, however, under his son Zahir Shah, until 1973, when his cousin Sirdar Mohammad Daud removed him, appointing himself the first president of the country.

During his four decades of power, Zahir Shah managed to keep a balance between competing regional superpowers - first between Britain and the USSR and later between the USA and the USSR. During the cold war Afghanistan was neutral, but slightly pro-Soviet so as to mollify the powers all around it. The Western alliance accepted this status quo, partly because of the absence of a better alternative.

But during the 1970s oil boom the newly installed President Daud was wooed by the West, through the intercession of the Shah of Iran and Saudi Arabia. He consequently planned to dispose of the small but influential Communist Party, which had made deep inroads in the labour and student sectors. (This probably would have meant also taking on the Afghan air force, which was trained in Russia and sympathetic to the Communist cause.) Before Daud could strike, however, the marxist People's Democratic Party of Afghanistan (PDPA), led by Nur Muhammad Taraki, bombarded the palace, killing Daud and his family and capturing power in 1978. Taraki, and later on Hafizullah Amin, made the same mistake as Amanullah, of trying to revolutionise the hyper-conservative Afghans overnight, and this did not go down very well with the populace. The Russians, for their part, were not happy with the way Amin had removed Taraki, or the fast pace of his daring reforms. When Amin started flirting with China and the Americans, the Soviet army moved in to depose him. They put their own man, Babrak Karmel, in power, along with their forces to protect him. The Americans, who had also been active since the communist coup in Kabul through Pakistan and its intelligence services, then stepped up their own interference. One can say that this was the moment of the launch of the Afghan Jihad, which is the root cause of present day terrorism.

Ever since the fall of the Ottoman Empire after the first world war, some Muslim rulers and intellectuals have lamented the abolition of the Caliphate and dreamed of Umma, a united world organisation of Muslims. There are two main international organisations of Muslims, the Islamic Conference (OIC) an association of states that encompasses all the Muslim majority countries, and the World Muslim Congress, which has no real teeth. There are however many less official organisations attempting to promote Muslim unity and to create links between Muslims in different countries.

'when the Taliban entered Kabul in triumph, the local CIA chief from the American Embassy in Islamabad was there to greet them'

During the last quarter of the twentieth century an ideology of jihad was strenuously promoted in the madrassas (religious schools) of Pakistan and Afghanistan and in the guerilla camps - with the generous help of American, British and Saudi military and intelligence advisers. These formed the nucleus of what is now called Al-Qaeda. Ironically, Blair now calls their ideology an ideology of evil. This is because a key difference today is that the devotees now rashly but logically (according to their logic) include Britain and USA, along with Russia, on their list of enemies. Osama bin Laden was the major figure in this set-up, along with the supporters whom the cause attracted from all over the Muslim world. He took the credit for defeating the Soviet troops in Afghanistan. During this period of trumped-up holy war there was a moment when President Carter's National Security Advisor Zbigniew Brzezinsky, looking over the hills of Afghanistan towards the USSR, commented to the satisfaction of the jihadis who were with him that it was there that the godless people lived - to the chorus of Allahu Akbar, 'GOD IS GREAT'. This strange brew created a new type of Umma, very different from what had been imagined by the old dreamers. A new crop arose of mindless and passionate devotees, totally prepared to kill and die. They were esteemed at the time by Western powers involved in the area as a greater ally than any potential secular supporters.

Money, arms, stinger missiles and every type of modern equipment poured in to these recruits from all over the Muslim world to stoke their holy war against the infidel invader. The ideology of Jihad was used to motivate these young zealots from many Muslim areas, who, with their American and British advisers, ultimately defeated the Soviet forces. These militant Islamists and their leaders were intoxicated with the belief that they alone had defeated the Soviet empire. Pakistan had been the major centre of the anti-Soviet forces, and its proliferating madrassas were the chief recruiting grounds. In these indoctrination factories, innocent youth were brainwashed by mullahs to be ready to go to heaven for the cause. These recruits, over the course of time, have hardened and matured, and they now are the indoctrinaters of a small but significant portion of a new generation of Muslims who are responsible for atrocities all over the world. They feel it is their duty to change the world according to their ideology.

After the withdrawal of Soviet forces in 1988, Sardar Najibullah (who had replaced Karmel as leader of the PDPA) remained in power in Kabul, though he had lost the control of the countryside. He was keen to come to some settlement with both the West and Pakistan, which was the conduit for all the armaments and men to the battlefront. He was plainly prepared to go along with any deal which could retain the secular character of the Afghan regime, but the Pakistani and American governments scorned him. Najibullah told a delegation of the Pakistani left that they were trying to demolish the Kabul regime with the help of the most reactionary and fundamentalist forces, which would take over Kabul and destroy it. He warned that once his regime was demolished, its debris would fall all over Pakistan - and it did. Islamists took Kabul, arrested Najibullah, imprisoned him in the UN compound, started a civil war among themselves and destroyed Kabul. After the Russian withdrawal the Western governments had largely washed their hands of the area. Pakistan was now left alone to solve the thorny problem of its wild neighbour.

With the active connivance of Western governments, Pakistan opted to back the Taliban. These 'students of Islamic knowledge' captured Kabul in 1996, and when they entered the city triumphantly the local CIA chief from the American embassy in Islamabad was there to welcome them. They established the most ruthless Sharia regime imaginable and thereby created a new kind of 'law and order' for Afghanistan. They publicly executed Najibullah and left his body hanging on a pole. The USA was pleased because it believed that once there was peace they could put an oil pipeline from Central Asia through Afghan territory. Furthermore, the Taliban were Sunni fundamentalists and thus were anti-Shia, which is to say against Iran as well. That was a considerable bonus for the American authorities (though, after 9/11, they pretended they had loathed the regime all along). A Taliban delegation even visited Houston as guests of the UNOCAL oil corporation. Activist women in the United States, though, were not happy that the regime's sharia laws were so harsh on Afghan women. The Pakistanis, however, were delighted because they were, in effect, the influential godfather of the Taliban.

However, the jihad continued in other places, and after the Al-Qaeda bombings in Kenya and elsewhere, the American government finally demanded that Osama be handed over to them as the man responsible for these crimes. Soon 9/11 changed the whole scene. America bombarded and bribed Afghanistan, coalition forces quickly took possession of the country and a new ruling arrangement was put in place. President Musharraf was made an offer he could not refuse - to join the alliance. A new experiment is now going on in Afghanistan under Hamid Karzai, while the radical Muslims have escaped into the mountains and fanned out along the borders of Pakistan.

The effects of the jihad on Pakistan

One result of this history is that Pakistan society has been gradually radicalised. For the first time, fundamentalist parties have established a large presence in parliament and a few of them have their own militant wings.

From 1988 to 1999 Pakistan experienced what could, with some charity, be called a democratic period. Nawas Sharif of the Muslim League and Benazir Bhutto of the People's Party alternated rule. Each of these was twice dismissed for pilfering from the state; and each presided over heartily corrupt regimes and pandered to the religious groups. General Baber, the interior minister under Benazir Bhutto, was the key patron of the Taliban, while Nawas Sharif flirted with bringing a Taliban style of rule into Pakistan itself. Their respective regimes retained volatile majorities in the house through ample and open patronage and bribes, until they were finally dismissed. Now Benazir Bhutto is a fugitive from justice and Nawas is in exile while loudly promoting democracy in Pakistan. President Musharraf came to power through a coup in 1999, though he has since tried to gain some legitimacy.

Pakistani politicians customarily curry favour with the Americans, who oblige them when the need arises. These politicians or their minions pay frequent visits to the USA, and subsequent contacts with even minor American functionaries of the State Department are announced so as to give the impression that they are important allies of the superpower. They manage their parties virtually through remote control. The People's Party and Muslim League remain the two major parties of Pakistan at the moment, but they have no mass base; it is largely through press manipulations that the rival leaders are trying to survive. In addition to these, there are the religious parties, who fought the national election of 2002 jointly, and had great success in the Afghan frontier province and in Baluchistan. The other significant party is the MQM, which represents migrants of Indian origin in Sindh. Pakistan political culture has a tradition of members defecting from one party to the other, particularly if that party is a party of government. President Musharraf rules with the support of factions of the Muslim League, the People's Party and the MQM. All this adds up to a political and cultural climate where there is no major force that can counter the fundamentalists.

Mullahs effectively rule the two frontline provinces - in one through coalition with the Muslim League, and in the other through a majority. Here they keep making noises and tabling bills to install Sharia laws, but these measures have so far been blocked. Still, there is no serious debate to counter the Mullahs' rhetoric in the mosques or in the religious seminaries. Islamic parties in the Pakhtun areas have absorbed Pakhtun nationalism along with their code of ethics, which reflects Sharia inclinations (but there are signs that the seminaries who were training militants have now stopped doing so). Until the elections of 2002 the Awami National Party was the only genuine secular social democratic organisation in the area, but it too became a victim of the growth of fundamentalism. Mullahs routed the party in the frontier province in which it had developed as part of the fight for independence from the British. At the moment MQM is the only party which is taking the mullahs head on both inside and outside parliament. Musharraf most certainly is a secular general, but there is no central planning to deal with terrorism in his regime. There are only ad hoc attempts to arrest or kill the terrorists, and the banning of terrorist organisations from time to time, when the US pressures them to do so. (However, Musharraf has taken tough action in South Waziristan and other border areas where mujahidin from foreign countries are reportedly hiding. He has been able to hand over Khalid Mohamad and others to the American authorities.)

Musharraf's position is made much more difficult when there are incidents such as reports in the press of the maltreatment of Pakistani prisoners in Guantanamo Bay. And the private channels that have been granted licenses play religious tunes and discuss Islam most of the time, which is also unhelpful in creating a secular climate (though the state media does not promote Jihad or religious fundamentalism). On top of all this, the fall-out from the Afghan jihad has created deep and pervasive social problems in Pakistan. A 'Kalashnikov culture' has come into being, alongside massive quantities of drugs, and this undermines law and order. It was only during the Taliban period, ironically, that poppy cultivation was banned in Afghanistan. Now it is back with full force and afflicting Pakistani society as well.

Organisations like Sipahe Sahaba (army of the prophet's friends) and Jaish Mohd (battalion of the prophet) are certainly involved in terrorist activities. Their victims are usually members of the Shia or Christian communities. Recently there have been a number of attacks on churches. A hostel for nuns and a school for girls run by missionaries were burned down. In 2005 the shrine of Bari Imam, where both Muslim sects used to visit, was attacked and nineteen people, mostly Shias, were killed. The fanatical philosophy of Bin Laden and the Sunni fundamentalists does not even tolerate visits to the shrines of Sufi saints, because they deem mysticism to be heresy. Two of the assassination attempts on Musharraf are thought to have stemmed from Al-Qaeda, under the direction of Bin Laden's chief lieutenant al Zawahri.

The Army is also mired in a mini-civil war with the Baluchi Sirdars (tribal chiefs) in Baluchistan. Since the establishment of Pakistan, successive governments have appeased these Sirdars, through grants or bribes. No reforms have taken place in these areas, and whenever there is civil or military strife the chiefs' demands for government concessions increase.

Whenever suicide bombers attack in the West, Pakistan authorities obligingly and publicly begin crackdowns at home. After the July bombing in London, Musharraf expelled foreign students from the seminaries, even though the majority of them were not involved in any violent activities. Some militants were rounded up, but later on they were quietly released. Perhaps they are kept on a leash for a rainy day

The civil service once acted as a buffer between the rules and the ruled, but this too has gradually eroded, and over the years it has proved very difficult to sustain the kind civil society institutions necessary for democratic life. Pakistan inherited a first class civil service from the British colonial period, with honest and competent officers, though at the same time their underlying attitude was colonial and this too impeded the growth of democracy. As Pakistan was a by-product of the Indian independence movement there was no proper political party to govern either. Successive regimes, particularly those of Ayub Khan and Zulfiqar Bhutto, expelled hundreds of trained bureaucrats, allegedly to reform the service but without improving the lot of the ones left behind. In colonial days the district magistrate was an effective institution; it was a pivot of administration. Today, however, unlike in colonial times, few government officers can resist a corrupt politician or the authority of the feudal leaders in the countryside. The old magistracy was given a coup de grace by the present regime, who have brought in elected mayors, or Nazims, in its place. But these have come mainly from the feudal and moneyed classes, and have no experience and no neutrality. Abolition of the district magistrate post has therefore destroyed the old buffer between the ruler and the ruled. These half-hearted and mindless reforms have demoralised the civil service, resulting in a deterioration of administration. Another problem has been the militarisation of the civil service. More ex-army officers are being appointed on civilian jobs of every kind, as if they had been trained for them.

In spite of all this one doesn't hear much resentment against the government. One reason is that the political leadership opposed to Musharraf has no moral authority left, and the other reason is that the top echelons of the regime have not yet been exposed for corruption.

Disasters can have a peculiar way of transforming antagonistic situations into peaceful ones. Turks and Greeks came a bit closer after the earthquakes in their countries. Indonesians are settling the issue of independence with their rebel province Aceh after the Tsunami devastated coastal areas at the end of 2004. Pakistan has just suffered one of the worst tragedies in its short history, the disaster in Kashmir, which resulted in the death of seventy thousand people, more than all who have died fighting Jihad since 1989 when the insurgency there started. One hopes perhaps that after the earthquake diplomacy will improve between India and Pakistan. Since Musharraf came to power talks to settle disputes with India had already been progressing, if slowly. However the suspicious mind-set in the two countries is ever at odds with a pragmatic and sane approach.

Indians were certainly among the first to offer help, but this was accepted only reluctantly. The army units and jihadi camps on the Pakistan side of Kashmir were all destroyed during the disaster, but Pakistan was not keen to allow Indian pilots to fly their helicopters over the area. There are some religious groups working to help victims, along with other volunteers, but at the same time they have been involved in verbal and physical abuses against each other. In spite of all this, however, the Kashmir issue is on its last legs. It has been internationalised in a way that nobody could anticipate. Like Pakistani groups, Indian Kashmiris are coming to help their relatives after fifty years. The erstwhile infidels from America and from Cuba are also helping the suffering community. It is quite likely that all these minglings between helpers and victims will soothe the politics of the area. Tragic events are a big leveller.

Two hundred Cuban doctors and paramedics arrived within a week of the earthquake to look after the needy and deprived, bringing in tons of medicines and surgical equipment, and are present in the areas where they are needed. At a meeting of international donors, Cuban deputy foreign minister Bruno Rodriguez made a moving speech, which stirred the world's conscience and warned that if help did not come quickly, many more would die. He pointed out that international help had been slow and insufficient and gave some appalling statistics: 'Every year, the industrialised world spends one trillion US dollars on weapons and another one trillion on advertisements; 400 billion on illicit drugs, 105 billion on alcoholic drinks; 17 billion on pet food and 12 billion on perfumes.' He noted that the rich world charges 436 billion dollars in debt servicing every year and another 100 billion in tariffs from the poor countries. He then observed, 'I have witnessed the pain and suffering of the humblest people'. President Musharraf was visibly touched by his speech, thanking him and asking him to convey his respect to Castro. Pakistanis in general were also delighted to hear what he said, perhaps being reminded that godless people after all are not so bad.

Unfortunately, we have suffered too many doses of fundamentalism since the Afghan war. Iqbal Ahamad reminds us of an image from a television screen in 1985.[1] 'On the White House lawn President Ronald Reagan is introducing, with great fanfare, a group of Afghan men, all leaders of mujahidin, to the media [saying] gentlemen these are the men who are the moral equivalent of the founding fathers of America.' Thus spoke the leader of the biggest Western democracy, in helping to create the foul political climate which is a key cause of our troubles today. There have recently been reports in the Pakistani press that some American officials are currently in contact with the remnants of the Taliban, in order to bring them closer to President Karzai. Such mechanics may or may not be useful for the Afghan regime, but in Pakistan there is no doubt that such tactics will once more serve to boost the fundamentalist forces.

---

1. In an article in *Dawn*, quoted by Mahmood Mamdani in *Good Muslim Bad Muslim: America, the Cold War and the Roots of Terror*, Pantheon 2004.

Interdependence Day (ID) 1st July
'An invitation to participate, experiment, communicate'
@ Royal Geographical Society, London

ID considers new ways of debating and acting on the key challenges of environmental change and globalization. ID will curate a family of interventions that explore the theme, create some thinking space and catalyze new cultural responses. There will be wellknown speakers offering 'Declarations of Interdependence', a mini film festival, performances, interventions and a 'Doctor's Surgery' where you can book an appointment to diagnose and discuss the world's problems.

Tickets are £6. Please send a cheque payable to 'The Open University' to Jan Smith, Geography Discipline, Faculty of SocialSciences, The Open University, Walton Hall, Milton Keynes MK7 6AA (j.h.smith@open.ac.uk). ID is the result of collaboration between organizations and individuals that are committed to better public understanding of environment and development issues.
www.interdependenceday.co.uk

Learning from Robert Mcnamara

Michael Rustin

Michael Rustin discusses Robert Mcnamara's
reassessments of his political life.

During the past twenty years, Robert S. McNamara, Secretary of Defence in
the Kennedy and Johnson Administrations from 1960 to 1968, has undertaken
a remarkable reappraisal of international events in which he was centrally
involved as a decision-maker and protagonist.[1] These events are the fire-
bombing of Japanese cities in 1945, culminating in the atomic bombs on
Hiroshima and Nagasaki, which McNamara states led to the total destruction
of 67 Japanese cities and the loss of 900,000 civilian Japanese lives; the Cuban
missile crisis of 1962, in which he says the world came within a hairsbreadth of
nuclear war; and the Vietnam war (1961-1973), which cost 3.8 million
Vietnamese and 58,000 American lives.

It is of course far from unusual for senior public figures to write memoirs
which describe their experience of the events in which they participated.
Commonly, the aim of such autobiographical writing is self-exculpatory,
clarifying and justifying the decisions taken by their authors when they were

---

1. The relevant works are: *In Retrospect: the Tragedy and Lessons of Vietnam* (1995);
   Argument without End: In Search of Answers to the Vietnam Tragedy (with James Blight
   and Robert Brigham, (1999); *Wilson's Ghost: Reducing the Risk of Conflict, Killing and
   Catastrophe in the 21st Century* (2001). See also James G. Blight and Janet M. Lang, *The
   Fog of War: Lessons from the Life of Robert S. McNamara* (2005), and Errol Morris's film,
   The Fog of War (2003).

in positions of power, though of course they often provide interesting inside information about events and their protagonists. What is exceptional about McNamara's writings, and the award-winning documentary film, *The Fog of War*, in which he is interviewed on camera about their substance, is that they set out dramatic reassessments of all of these events and, far from justifying McNamara's decisions and recommendations made at the time, propose that these were in major aspects greatly mistaken.

McNamara's reputation was always as the supreme technocrat, one who believed in the application of rational systems of decision-making to every problem he encountered. His single-mindedness in this respect is evident in these memoirs. It is documented in his role as analyst of the efficiency and effectiveness of American strategic bombing in the Second World War, in his work as Vice-President of the Ford Motor Company - in which he and his chosen staff modernised the management systems of an organisation whose managers at the time of his appointment were almost all non-graduates - and in his role as Secretary of Defence from 1960 to 1968. He was described by Walter Lippmann as not only the best Secretary of Defence in US history, but as the first who ever exercised civilian control over its military. (McNamara's conflicts with the generals, notably Curtis LeMay, is a continuing though discreetly described theme of his memoir.) As some readers will remember, in the campaigns against the Vietnam war, McNamara's apparently cold and calculating misuses of scientific methods for purposes of destruction were a frequent object of denunciation.

However, the commitment to reason and understanding which were the primary passion of McNamara's years in power have been put to a further use during his long years of subsequent reflection. (*In Retrospect* was published when he was 79, the interviews of *The Fog of War* were undertaken when he was 85; and his most recent book was published last year, when he was 89.) Is there a rational method, he has asked himself, by which we could come to better understand the events of the past, of which at the time we unavoidably had only a limited and one-sided knowledge? Using a 'critical oral history' approach - a method that he and colleagues at Harvard and Brown Universities developed - meetings were set up between the former protagonists of conflicts, in which the perspectives of former participants and enemies could be set against one another, and their testimony compared with the documentary records.[2] This was undertaken in two series of meetings with participants from the Cuban missile crisis and the Vietnam war. Senior figures from both sides took part (including Fidel Castro and the former Vietnamese Foreign Minister Nguyen Co Thach), and each side set out its view of what had taken place, or, in the case of the Cuban missile crisis, the catastrophe which had nearly taken place. It is this willingness to subject his earlier definitions of the situation to this test of independent reality and experience that gives McNamara's testimony its exceptional interest and authority.

McNamara learned in the investigations of the events of the Cuban missile crisis not only that 160 nuclear warheads had been placed in Cuba without the knowledge of the US, but also that Castro had firmly recommended to Krushchev their use to counter-attack the American mainland, in the event of the anticipated invasion of Cuba. McNamara describes himself going white with shock when Castro revealed this in one of their meetings, realising then as he had not before how extremely close the world had come to a nuclear catastrophe. (At this time, the argument in the White House was between those, mainly the military, who wished to launch an attack on Cuba, and those, including John F. Kennedy, Robert Kennedy and McNamara, who opposed this, though McNamara now ascribes the escape from disaster as having been so close as to have amounted to mere luck.) Nevertheless, McNamara gives large credit to the role in the discussion of the former US Ambassador in Moscow Llewellyn 'Tommy' Thompson, whose previous contact with and understanding of Krushchev enabled Kennedy to make positive decisions in responding to his messages.

It is the absence of any equivalent understanding of the North Vietnamese to which McNamara ascribes a great deal of responsibility for the disaster of the Vietnam war. (The parallels with Iraq are evident, though McNamara has consistently declined to comment directly on this or other contemporary events.) The framing of events which dominated the American approach to Vietnam, from Eisenhower onwards, was that of the Cold War, and the 'domino theory', which declared that the loss of South Vietnam to the Communists would threaten pro-Western regimes elsewhere in the region - Thailand,

---

2. For more on this go to www.WatsonInstitute.org and follow links to Projects and Global Security.

Malaysia, even India.[3] It is clear that McNamara was himself during those years caught up inextricably by this perspective, though he also understood the unwinnable situation of the war and the weakness and corruption of the South Vietnamese regime. His own plan, such as it was, was to impose such pressure on the North Vietnamese as would constrain them to negotiate a settlement, whilst seeking to minimise direct American military engagement, and above all to avoid the risk of a wider war with China or the USSR. But military pressure was ineffective, and negotiations in Paris and elsewhere made no progress. McNamara was urging a scaling-down of American involvement in 1968 when his disagreements with President Johnson led to his departure from the Administration.

McNamara has engaged in a prolonged reflection on the Vietnam war, which has led eventually to an understanding by him of the errors of perception and judgement which led to it. It is clear that his meetings with the Vietnamese were very significant in this process. He describes the deep gulf of understanding at the first angry meetings with his former adversaries. McNamara rejected as 'absurd' their definition of American aims as colonialist, while the Vietnamese refuted the American framing of the conflict in ideological, Cold War terms, instead insisting that theirs had been foremost a struggle for national self-determination. Don't you realise, said Dao Huy Ngoc to McNamara, that by 1945 we already had four thousand years of history. We had fought the Chinese, the Japanese and the French for our independence, and did not see ourselves as anyone's puppets or instruments. McNamara came to understand, as he had not before, the full extent of Vietnamese commitment to their struggle, which they declared they had been willing to continue at *any* human and material cost. This, he now saw, had made military victory for the US and its allies impossible; and he came to recognise the gulf of understanding which had doomed to failure the recurrent attempts at negotiations.

McNamara seems now clear that that the Vietnam war should not have been fought, and that the settlement that was made after the American defeat and withdrawal could and should have been negotiated at a much earlier stage. He sees the Geneva Accords of 1954 (which the US refused to ratify) as a

---

3. For more on this war, including McNamara's role, see Kurt Jacobsen's article in this issue.

crucial missed opportunity;[4] and states, in *On Retrospect*, that the Americans could and should have withdrawn from Vietnam in 1963, 1964, or 1965. He reports Kennedy's commitment to withdrawal of American personnel from Vietnam just prior to his assassination, and indicates his belief that if Kennedy had remained President the war might have been avoided. But McNamara did remain Secretary of Defence under Lyndon Johnson for several years, and in that role he had a large responsibility for the conduct of the war in Vietnam. Whether or not Kennedy could have escaped the logic of the Cold War and its simplistic domino theory, it is clear that McNamara on his own did not. It is what happened after the American defeat, after which no other Asian dominoes fell, and perhaps the end of the Cold War itself, which has now enabled McNamara to extricate himself from this frame of thinking, and to imagine a course of history in which the tragedy of the Vietnam war did not take place.

I n his role as a senior administrator in the United States government, Robert McNamara was directly involved in actions which led to enormous and deliberate losses of human life. This is a common factor of his experience as a strategic analyst of the US bombing of Japan, and as Secretary of Defence. He does not seek to evade his own responsibilities for those actions, though of course he makes clear that these were not his alone. It is moving to see and hear, in the *Fog of War*, McNamara's reflections on the catastrophic destruction brought to Japanese cities by fire-bombing of which he was himself an instrument, and his noting that in both his own and General Curtis LeMay's view, these actions would have been judged as war-crimes had the Allies lost the war - justly as he gives us reason to understand. It is necessary to follow the rule of proportionality in war, he suggests, as the Allies did not. Such admissions of responsibility are rare indeed.

How does McNamara live with his conscience, many have asked, including some critics in the period after the publication of his retrospective writings: this is all too little, too late. Why doesn't he apologise for all the harm that he has done? Why did he not support the anti-war movement after his resignation as Secretary of Defence (since we know that even then he shared many of its doubts about the war, which continued under Nixon and Kissinger for a further

4. This history was explored in the critical oral history US-Vietnamese Dialogue, described in *Argument Without End*.

five years)? Why does he not now either make or support direct criticism of the Bush Administration, which is violating virtually all of the principles for the conduct of international affairs that he now upholds so vigorously, in his late eighties? But others have been appreciative of the truth-seeking quality of his recent writings. *On Retrospect* was translated and widely read in Vietnam after its publication, and it was this memoir that made Vietnamese leaders willing to meet with him to explore the events of the war. Anne Morrison Welsh, widow of Norman Morrison, the Quaker who burnt himself to death in protest against the war underneath McNamara's Pentagon office window, wrote to him to express her appreciation of his candour.

One might best understand McNamara's position by reference to the view he takes of the responsibilities of public servants, who, as he points out, are non-elected, and whose obligation is to serve their elected governments to the best of their ability. Inherent in the role of public servants, especially in times of war, is the necessity to take decisions that will have terrible consequences for human lives. McNamara holds to an ethic of responsibility.[5] He is exceptional in the starkness with which he acknowledges the scale of the consequences of the decisions he has been involved in, and in his disinclination to minimise these. He sees his recent investigations and writings as maintaining his lifelong commitment to reason, by which he seeks to serve what he sees as the public - indeed now universal human - interest. This he now defines as the preservation of peace and the avoidance in the new century of the catastrophic scale of death and injury of the twentieth century in which he participated as a powerful decision-maker.[6]

Many political memoirs exploit the fascination of the public with the hidden world of power from which they are normally excluded. McNamara offers rather little of this kind - he is notably without rancour towards

---

5. One is reminded of Max Weber's 'ethic of responsibility', set out in his famous essay *Politics as a Vocation* (1919) in which he sets out the morality which requires that practical possibilities be taken account of, in contrast to a morality of absolute values. These two kinds of moral judgements lastingly divide those who accept political responsibility, in practice or in mind, and those who refuse it, instead preferring to subject its outcomes to uncompromised moral assessment. It is common for this division to become an uncomprehending and destructive kind of psychological splitting on both sides.

6. McNamara is a forceful advocate of nuclear disarmament. See, for example, his 'Apocalypse Soon', *Foreign Policy* May-June 2005, www.foreignpolicy.com.

former colleagues and opponents (Henry Cabot Lodge is an exception) -
and his writings are focused on what needs to be known to learn from these
past events, and the errors of judgement which brought them about. His
lack of interest in self-exculpation can be seen in the virtual omission from
his memoirs of his years as President of the World Bank, and, perhaps more
importantly, of his role as Secretary of Defence in developing the strategic
doctrine of Mutual Assured Destruction (in which neither side in the Cold
War would seek a first strike capacity and thus be tempted, as the American
generals at one point were, to launch a pre-emptive nuclear war) - which
he saw as reducing the risk of nuclear disaster. My own surmise is that a
major reason for McNamara's capacity to live in good faith with the
consequences of his actions is his belief that his efforts to avert nuclear
war, in alliance with both Presidents Kennedy and Johnson, were significant
in their effects, and that in this sense his 'accomplishments' (to which he
refers without explication) outweigh even the huge losses of life in which
he was implicated.

Contemporary lessons from history

What lessons can we draw for contemporary politics from McNamara's
testimony? This is not an easy question to answer. It is fortunate that
McNamara has had such a long active life, since it has enabled him to become
a genuine historian of his own times. Still-active politicians worry about the
consequences of knowledge and understanding for their own power and
reputation, and for this reason fear and resist open investigation. For a
historian, such as McNamara has become - as have those who joined him in
investigating the Cuban missile crisis, the Vietnam war, and the breakdown
of US-Soviet détente - these are no longer factors of consequence. Indeed it
may be that it has been in order to preserve a sphere of independence of
judgement, and to keep partisanship and its aversions to reason at bay, that
McNamara has declined to become involved, even in the obvious application
of his 'eleven lessons' to contemporary events such as the Iraq War.

The South African Truth and Reconciliation Commission has been an
emblematic institutional innovation following the overthrow of the apartheid
regime in South Africa - though its procedure was confined to the investigation
of cases of individual abuse, and threw little or no light on the decision-making

of those who held power in the regime, or among its opponents. The insuperable difficulties which the TRC experienced in taking its search for truth beyond the experience of fairly lowly individuals shows the problems that would be found in attempting to apply to South Africa - or to other contemporary events and crises - the 'critical oral history' method of investigation.

However, even if open truth-seeking of this kind is beyond the capacities or inclinations of most politicians (in virtue of their interests and roles, as much as of limitations of character), it might be that some substitute could be created by those a little further from the action - perhaps in the spirit of the 'teach-ins', which, during the period of the Vietnam war, did at times achieve genuine debate. This debate depended

'the demonisation of enemies as alien kinds of immoral being is one of the main enemies of rational judgement'

on the participation in these exchanges of supporters as well as opponents of that war, something that was made easier by the fact that Britain was not in fact a combatant (though the Wilson government's rhetorical commitment to the war at the time made it feel otherwise).

Could one envisage an investigation of the Iraq war in which supporters and opponents would aim to clarify the assumptions and beliefs that led to it, and to reassess these in the light of what we now know? Could 'expert witnesses' be found and called? Participants would need to be drawn from many countries, including Iraq. Such an inquiry would investigate a history long pre-dating the Iraq War itself, just as the understanding of Vietnam needed to go back to the end of the World War Two and the defeat of Japan. Could the invasion of Kuwait by Iraq have been avoided? Was the imposition of economic sanctions an appropriate punishment of Iraq following its defeat in the first Gulf War? What other options were and are available for bringing about the liberalisation of tyrannies such as that of Saddam Hussein - options that might involve less damage and suffering to the people living under such regimes? What assumptions should have been made about the consequences of the military overthrow of Saddam, given we can now see that the regime embodied the rule of a minority Sunni population over a much larger Shia majority? What part have assumptions about the security and interests of Israel played in calculations about the dangers posed by Iraq, and indeed Iran, in the Middle East? What importance should be attached to the threat of 'global terrorism' in policy-making, and how can one differentiate between the psychological consequences of 9/11, together with the mobilisation of anxiety for political purposes, and the real and potential risks signified by the events of that day? What part does access to and control of oil supply play in these decisions, and how realistic in any case is it to seek to manage the flow of oil by military means, given that it is only of value to its producers if someone will buy it at a market price? What if any good outcomes might now be realistically anticipated from the war, and how should they be balanced against the damage it has caused?

McNamara's testimony shows us that the issues underlying conflicts are always complex, and at the time involve large elements of ignorance and error. Further, that decisions are best based on the belief that opponents as well as ourselves are rational in the pursuit of their own interests. One must therefore learn to understand how they conceive their own interests, to put oneself in their shoes. ('Empathise with your enemy' is McNamara's term for this.) Although he does not say this, the demonisation of enemies as alien kinds of immoral being - and the mobilisation of horror stories to justify this view - is one of the main enemies of rational judgement. It is not that the horror stories, for example concerning Saddam Hussein's rule, are not sometimes true, but that there are many kinds of death and suffering, and those inflicted by ourselves in supposed good faith may be as harmful in their consequences - or more harmful - as those inflicted by our apparently evil enemies.[7] The crucial question about the Iraq War is thus not 'did Saddam Hussein morally deserve to be overthrown', but how should one balance the costs of one set of actions - the invasion of Iraq - as they turned out, against what might otherwise have been decided during the sequences of events that included and preceded 9/11.

My belief is that the atmosphere of politics in Britain and the United States has been rendered toxic by Iraq, and by the complicity of governments in preventing rational exploration of the circumstances and consequences of the war. It is impossible to have belief in a democratic process in which so little

---

7. McNamara's reminder of the scale of devastation inflicted by the Allies in its terror-bombings of World War Two should caution us against the idea that our enemies live in a moral universe quite different from our own. The reason he does not denounce Castro for his admission that he had recommended nuclear counter-attack against the United States could be that he knew that his own side was committed to a similar position.

respect is given to the truth. Everything which the New Labour government now does has been tarnished by the evasions which continue to accompany its role in the Iraq crisis. It may be that mutual disillusionment between Tony Blair and many in the Labour Party is what lies behind Blair's ever-more embattled pursuit of his 'reforming agenda', a long-standing truce and compromise between Blair and his adopted party having seemingly broken down. It is impossible to 'move on from the war', as we are often asked to do, until and unless some accounting of what has happened is made, and responsibilities (not necessarily the same thing as blame) for judgements and errors are assigned.

How is this to be accomplished? A process of investigation and debate is needed, in which those who have held and still hold different views take part. McNamara and his colleagues' investigations of the events of the 1960s provide us with an example of how it is possible to bring reason to bear on issues of this kind. What is needed is to translate those procedures, which focused on the events of a generation past, into an exploration of the history of the near present-day.

London inside-out

Doreen Massey

*Doreen Massey argues that we need to be more
aware of the role of London in producing corporate
globalisation.*

In the numbed days after the first bombs went off on London's public transport in
July 2005, Ken Livingstone said 'this city is the future'. 'This city' he said 'typifies
what I believe is the future of the human race and a future where we grow together
and we share and we learn from each other' (GLA press release, 8.7.05).

He set London in the wider context of the development of European cities
generally, and of cities around the world:

> If you go back a couple of hundred years to when the European cities really
> started to grow and peasants left the land to seek their future in the cities
> there was a saying that 'city air makes you free' and the people who have
> come to London, all races, creeds and colours, have come for that. This is a
> city that you can be yourself as long as you don't harm anyone else. You can
> live your life as you choose to do rather than as somebody else tells you to
> do. It is a city in which you can achieve your potential. It is our strength and
> that is what the bombers seek to destroy ...
>
> This year for the first time in human history a majority of people live in
> cities. London continues to grow and I say to those who planned this dreadful
> attack whether they are still here in hiding or somewhere abroad, watch next
> week as we bury our dead and mourn them, but see also in those same days
> new people coming to this city to make it their home to call themselves
> Londoners and doing it because of that freedom to be themselves ... (ibid).

Livingstone's passion sounded out in stark contrast to the manufactured sincerity of Tony Blair. Nor did Ken speak of good and evil, but of a real grounded politics. His commitment to diversity and hospitality rang a clear note after a general election, some months previously, in which dismally negative debates about immigration and asylum had been prominent.

Nor were these sentiments without a basis on the streets. Surveys show Londoners consistently valuing the city's cultural and ethnic mix and seeing that as central to London's identity.[1] The *Guardian*, earlier that year, had published a special supplement: 'London: the world in one city: a special celebration of the most cosmopolitan place on earth' (21.01.05). In the aftermath of the bombing the London *Evening Standard* ran a special edition with the title 'London United', and in *Time Out* ('London's weekly listings bible') the front cover said simply 'Our City'. At the gathering in Trafalgar Square Ben Okri read a poem he had re-titled 'A hymn to London': 'Here lives the great music of humanity' (*Evening Standard*, 15.7.05). The Olympic Bid had been built around claims of cultural and ethnic diversity; there is the Respect (now Rise) campaign against racism. Nor has this been only a simplistic version of multiculturalism, a claim to some happy harmony - Livingstone's stance since the bombing has been firm in its refusal to bow to pressures for exclusion and repression, and in its determination to continue with criticism where this is thought politically to be warranted. It recognises that this may be a conflictual negotiation of place.

There is evidently much more that could be said about this, and Ken personally has gone to great lengths in thinking through these issues. Indeed in the months after the bombing 'multiculturalism' became again a contested term. It is also important to register that such statements ('This city is the future'), in the singularity of the future to which they lay claim, could themselves be seen as an imperialising gesture - our future is the universal future. (It is in fact only one possible future, and even if it comes to pass for London and for other places, it may nonetheless exist in a world in which there are other futures too.) I would prefer to read such words, therefore, as a statement of political commitment. Not just as a description, nor as a claim to

---

1. See, for instance, MORI, 2004, *What is a Londoner?* 2 April 2004; Research for the Commission on London Governance.

be at the front of some posited singular historical queue, but as a statement that London stands for something, a particular *kind* of future, but carrying with it the possibility that this may be one future in a still varied and plural world. Maybe other places, other cities, will be different.

At the moment, however, I just want to draw out one point, which is that this positive attitude towards diversity is claimed to be central to London's identity; is something that a majority of Londoners seem to be quite proud of (and this without ignoring the evident racisms and intolerances which abound); and is to some extent embedded in policy and often drawn upon and celebrated in the arts. It is one of the ways (and in the period around the bombing the dominant way) in which London thinks of itself as a 'world city'. Moreover it is politically interesting - and heartening - because it is a claim to place that is open rather than bounded, hospitable rather than excluding, ever-changing rather than eternal. And nothing that follows is meant to gainsay that.

***

What I should like to explore about this imagination of place held by so many Londoners, however, is how it might be broadened out.

First of all this is an internal, indeed internalised, view of the city. It is about hospitality, about those who come to 'us', about the strangers within the gate. It calls to Derrida's notion of *villes-franches*.[2] And that is excellent. However the geographies of places aren't only about what lies within them. A richer geography of place acknowledges also the connections that run out from 'here': the trade-routes, investments, political and cultural influences; power-relations of all sorts run out from here around the globe and link the fate of other places to what is done in London. This is the other geography - the 'external geography' of a place. It is a geography that attaches to any place, but it is especially important to a place like London.

In recent debates about identity we have moved away from notions of isolated individuals towards an understanding of identity as thoroughly relational, as constructed through rather than prior to our interactions with others. The same move has been made in relation to place-identity. And yet the way that this

---

2. J. Derrida, *On cosmopolitanism and forgiveness*, Routledge, London 2001.

insight has been developed has often been to concentrate on the implications for the internal constructions of identity: the internal multiplicities and fragmentations, and so forth. And so it has been with place-identity too: it is a commonplace now that every place is hybrid, that we must be critical of notions of coherent communities. This too is a positive move (except when it is repeated as a mantra without consideration of the real difficulties and complexities it implies). Yet there is another geography, that geography of external relations on which identities, including the identities of places, depend. How do we bring *that* into our attitude to, and our politics of, place?

This tendency to inwardlookingness becomes even clearer when we turn to my second reservation about the characterisation of London as multicultural future of the world. For London is not *only* multicultural. It is also - for instance - a heartland of the production, command and propagation of what we have come to call neoliberal globalisation. Indeed it was in London that many of its lineaments were first conceived. The City (capital C), and all the vast and intricate cultural and economic infrastructure that surrounds it, is crucial to neoliberalism. About 30 per cent of the daily global turnover of foreign exchange takes place in London; London has over 40 per cent of the global foreign equity market; 70 per cent of all eurobonds are traded in London ... and so on. Meanwhile, the 2005 UN Report on Human Development produces 'the usual' statistics - the kind that are so bad it is difficult to know how to receive them. The world's richest 500 people own more wealth than the poorest 416 million. And it is not just a problem of the super-rich: Europeans spend more on perfume each year than the $7billion needed to provide 2.6 billion people with access to clean water. London is a crucial node in the production of an increasingly unequal world. When Ken Livingstone speaks of people coming to this city because of the freedom it offers 'to be themselves' he is right. But people find their way here for other reasons too. They come because of poverty and because their livelihoods have disappeared in the maelstrom of neoliberal globalisation (and millions more are left behind). And it has to be at least a question as to whether London is a seat of some of the causes of these things.

And that raises in turn the question of what is our responsibility for those wider geographies of place. Most formulations of the relation between 'local place' and globalisation imagine local places as *products* of globalisation ('the global production of the local'). It is a formulation that easily slides into a conceptualisation of the local as *victim* of globalisation. Here globalisation figures as some sort of external agent that arrives to wreak havoc on local places. And often indeed it is so. The resulting politics in consequence often resolves into strategies for 'defending' local places against the global. Such strategies always tend to harbour a host of political ambiguities, but in the case of London (and of places like London - of which, to varying degrees, there are many) this simple story just cannot hold. For London is one of those places in which capitalist globalisation, with its deregulation, privatisation, 'liberalisation', is produced. Here we have also 'the local production of the global'.

And yet a celebration of multiculturalism and a politics of anti-racism exist alongside a persistent obliviousness on the part of the majority of Londoners to the external relations - the daily global raiding parties, the activities of London's financial sector and multinationals - upon which the very character and existence of London depend.

The current London Plan provides a case in point.[3] Here, in consideration specifically of the city's economy, London's identity as a world city is understood in terms of its financial power. Moreover this global financial muscle is presented as a simple achievement. It is not reflected-upon in its intimate relation to imperialism and colonialism.[4] The Plan presents no critical analysis of the global power-relations that sustain this world-citydom; it does not follow those relations out around the world and ask what they may be responsible for; it asks no questions about the connections between this economic power and the increasing inequalities around the world. Indeed, the Plan has as its central economic aim the expansion of London as a global financial power. It must be stressed that in this the London Plan is not at all unusual. *This is the norm.* Thinking about places, including plans for places, nearly always in this sense remains 'within the place'. It is part of the tension between a territorialised politics and a world structured also by flows. But what it means is that, in this city which is indeed in so many ways progressive and

3. Greater London Authority, *The London Plan: Spatial Development Strategy for Greater London*, Greater London Authority, London 2004.
4. A. King, *Global cities: post-imperialism and the internationalization of London*, Routledge, London 1990.

even radical, we have, we nurture, the production of the beast itself.

(And yet most of the local criticism of this Plan has focused - not wrongly but perhaps too narrowly - on the effects it will have within the city itself.)

Ken spoke, in his address on 8 July, of that now well-known fact that now 'for the first time in human history a majority of people live in cities'. In part that massive urbanisation is a product of the current form of globalisation; indeed cities are crucial in a host of ways to the neoliberal project. But they figure in very diverse ways within it. The biggest growth in the urban population has been in the global South, and in the 'planet of slums' that Mike Davis has documented with such power.[5] Such places are precipitates of the selfsame processes that have helped London to 'reinvent itself' (London Plan, p13) since the decline of the 1970s and 1980s. Is this, then, another side of London as 'the future of the world'? Does London also stand for this?

***

How might a politics of place beyond place be imagined? What follows are just a few thoughts, but they do draw on many campaigns and arguments already under way. Indeed, it should be said at the start that the overwhelming prioritisation of the financial City and its attendant sectors that characterised the initial version of the London Plan has already been somewhat muted in response to criticism at the Scrutiny Committee (set up by the GLA to hear opinions on the Plan), from almost all parts of the political spectrum. The *reasons* for the criticism varied, from the dangers of becoming too reliant on one economic sector to the inequalities, both spatial and social, that such a unique prioritisation engenders within the metropolitan area itself. London is the most unequal place in the UK, but that internal inequality is intimately linked to its economic structure and its global role. As far as I know, however, there was no criticism of the priorities of the Plan that focused on the global effects of that global role. The concentration was on effects within the city itself.

There are, moreover, some ways in which the London Plan does exhibit both this outwardlooking perspective and a recognition that London is a cause

5. M. Davis, 'Planet of slums', *New Left Review*, No 26, 2004; UN-Habitat, *The challenge of the slums*, London 2003; UN-Habitat, *State of the world's cities 2004/2005*, World Urban Forum, Barcelona 2004.

of what happens in the wider world, as well as having to respond to its effects. This is the case in relation to climate change (and indeed environmental issues more generally): here it is stated that not only must policy manage the impacts of climate change on London but it must also work to reduce London's own contribution to the production of that problem. The Food Strategy, similarly, pays attention to the global effects of London's food consumption and argues explicitly that responsibility be taken for these impacts - in terms of resources, food miles, waste disposal and so forth - and for promoting a wider consciousness of, and respect for, all elements in the global food-chain. In these ways, London's emerging strategies indicate what might be done.

A strategy that acknowledges the global effects that emanate from London should not, anyway, be all down to the city government; rather, what is crucially at issue is how we conceive of, and respond to the responsibilities of, our identities as 'Londoners' (or as members of any other place). There are, for instance, campaigns around particular parts of the economy that are important to London, and around particular companies that have their headquarters in London, but with a focus on their global roles. Oil and gas for instance: they account in one way and another for about a quarter of London's stock exchange; Shell and BP have headquarters in London; London is utterly dependent on oil. And a number of campaigns have focused on these facts, taking them as a starting point for wider arguments. There is, for instance, the project 'Unravelling the Carbon Web' organised by PLATFORM.[6] This includes a range of different projects, and aims to examine the oil industry and the sectors that serve it from a host of different angles, but with a focus on the role of London. A linked project is 'Remember Saro-Wiwa: the Living Memorial'.[7] This is a public art initiative to mark the tenth anniversary of the execution of Saro-Wiwa and it was given a big launch in Spring 2005, in City Hall, with an opening speech from the Mayor. It is not a 'memorial' that looks backwards; rather it is about raising awareness of the global implications of this city's oil dependence and its position as the site of so much petroleum power. There are many such campaigns, and they are small,

---

6. www.carbonweb.org and www.platformlondon.org.
7. www.remembersarowiwa.com. Campaigns around oil extraction in Ogoniland led to the execution of Ken Saro-Wiwa and eight colleagues. See Ken Wiwa, 'The murder of Ken Saro-Wiwa', *Soundings* 2, 1996.

but part of their aim is to look beyond the local place, to trace its implications around the world. Some projects link up with ecological campaigns. Some link particular communities within London to other parts of the world - people from the Nigerian community linking to the Saro-Wiwa project, for example. A way of thinking multiculturalism outwards.

Or again, it might be possible for there to be, within the ambit of the London Social Forum perhaps, a specific emphasis on solidarity with struggles in other parts of the world whose battles link back to companies that are based in London. One obvious possibility, since London was the birthplace of so much in the way of ideas about deregulation, would be links with campaigns against the enforced privatisation of utilities in the global South.

Perhaps, too, the Mayor and/or the London Assembly could themselves support alternative globalisations, help challenge the nature of the trade and financial arrangements through which the current form of globalisation operates. There is, for instance, the possibility of joining that growing alliance of city and regional authorities that refuse simply to go along with GATS regulations. 'GATS-free zones' are mushrooming in other countries in Europe. Or there is the issue of Fair Trade. There is, for instance, a Fair Trade Town and City campaign (Bristol is a member). But London is significant not only for drinking coffee but also as a place where coffee is traded. It was the radical GLC of the 1980s that established Twin Trading, a wholesaling organisation that took the city's fair-trade politics beyond the politics of consumption.[8] That same GLC was also supportive in a number of ways of the 'counterglobalisation' of the trades-union movement, aiding contact between workers in different parts of the world.

One final example, which encapsulates a number of the arguments I am trying to make. In part precisely because of the current way in which London is a world city it finds it very difficult to reproduce itself. Public-sector workers and lower-paid private-sector workers can barely survive, and a whole range of schemes has had to be devised to enable adequate recruitment. One thing that this means is that London is massively dependent

---

8. Although the Fairtrade Cities initiative of the Fairtrade Foundation itself necessarily goes beyond individualised consumption (this indeed is one of the points of organising at the level of place): see, for one discussion, Jo Littler's interview with Clive Barnett and Kate Soper, 'Consumers: agents of change?' in *Soundings* 31, 2005.

on labour from abroad, including from the global South. It is dependent, for instance, on health workers from Africa and Asia. These countries can ill-afford to lose such workers, and they have paid for their training. So India, Sri Lanka, Ghana, South Africa are subsidising the reproduction of London. It is a perverse subsidy, flowing to the rich from the poor.[9] This is a difficult issue because it can so easily be turned around into a racist denial of immigration rights. The Medact Report - which was concerned with the UK as a whole (and is referenced in note 9) - suggests, in relation to health workers from Ghana, that the two health systems (Ghanaian and British), including their trades-unions, could be thought of as one system and that the UK could pay restitution to the Ghanaian system for the perverse subsidy that currently flows in the opposite direction.

There may be other approaches. But this one is interesting because it changes what otherwise might be thought of as *aid* to Ghana, with all its connotations of conditionality and charity and the power relations thereby implied, into a matter of the fulfilment of an *obligation*.[10] It expressly addresses the issue of unequal external geographies. It is also important because, through this, it forces a re-imagination of place: it looks from the inside out; it recognises not just the outside within but also the 'inside' that lies beyond.

At the moment, however, this is not even a live political debate amongst Londoners. It is not an issue that has registered as integral to the identity of this place. We may celebrate the arrival of Ghanaians in London as part of the great ethnic mix. But we do not follow those lines of connection out around the rest of the world and enquire about the effects there. We need to globalise in some way that local claim to multiculturalism. All of the examples described here are small but such things are needed to help promote an outwardlookingness, a consciousness of the wider geographies and responsibilities of place. Moreover, *within* the place, within London, once such issues start to be raised, all of them would be disputed - which could only enrich the internal politics of place, multiply the lines of debate around

9. K. Mensah, M. Mackintosh and L. Henry, 'The "skills drain" of health professionals from the developing world: a framework for policy formulation', Medact, London 2005, www.medact.org/content/Skills%20drain/Mensah%20et%20al.%202005.pdf.

10. M. Mackintosh, 'Aid, restitution and international fiscal redistribution in health care: reflections in the context of rising health professional migration', Paper presented at Development Studies Association annual conference 7-9 September 2005.

which 'place' must be negotiated. It would challenge the current exoneration of 'the local' within a critical global politics, and begin to develop a local politics of place beyond place.

This article draws on talks given at the European Social Forum 2005, the Institute of Contemporary Arts as part of 'London Talks', a series accompanying the exhibition 'London in Six Easy Steps: Six Curators, Six Weeks, Six Perspectives', ICA London, 16 August-25 September 2005, and at the Café Diplo seminar series of Le Monde Diplomatique. The background theoretical arguments are set out in D. Massey, For Space, Sage 2005; and D. Massey, 'Geographies of responsibility', Geografiska Annaler, Vol 86B(1), 2004.

UNIVERSITY OF WALES INSTITUTE, CARDIFF | ATHROFA PRIFYSGOL CYMRU, CAERDYDD

INTERNATIONAL RESEARCH CONFERENCE

RECLAIMING THE ECONOMY

THE ROLE OF COOPERATIVE ENTERPRISE, OWNERSHIP AND CONTROL

UWIC, CARDIFF, 6-8 SEPTEMBER 2006

Alongside globalisation, the enterprise culture and the stakeholder economy, there is increasing evidence that cooperative and mutual forms of enterprise are spreading and developing across the world.

This international conference is designed to explore the profile of cooperative forms of organization with a view to establishing a multidisciplinary research agenda which serves the mutual interests of both academics and practitioners.

**For more information contact
Len Arthur on: 029 2041 6374 or**
email Molly Scott Cato: mscott-cato@uwic.ac.uk
www.uwic.ac.uk/ubs/conferences/

WIRC
Wales Institute for Research into Co-operatives
Athrofa Cymru ar gyfer Ymchwil i Gydweithfaoedd

UWIC
Cardiff's **metropolitan** university
prifysgol **metropolitan** Caerdydd

'Man's the Talk on Road'

A dialogue with young black people on their experiences of gun crime

Ejos Ubiribo

Ejos Ubiribo looks at the issues behind gun crime.

Before my own brother's murder in 2002 I was already very concerned about the slaughter of black British men at the hands of their own brothers. At any given opportunity I would raise these concerns, which more often than not would be on the phone in conversation with two of my girlfriends (the only two that kindly endured my marathon diatribes). In trying to make sense of the madness which for me was the near weekly accounts of the murder of black young males, I became conscious of the deep rooted apathy about this in both the black community and wider society. Black men killing black men did not matter. Feeling powerless I resigned myself to just talking about it. However, it is something that is extremely difficult to ignore when the accounts are of people you know.

My first experience of gun crime was in 1998 watching a news report of a young man gunned down in Willesden, north west London. Although barely catching the victim's surname, there was something familiar about it. Less than an hour later I learned that it was Rudy King, the cousin of a friend. Then in July 1999, my friend's boyfriend, Dean Roberts, was shot dead in Harlesden, again in north west London, three weeks before the birth of their son. In the following few years I came to know (both directly and indirectly) many young black males involved in shootings. But it was the beginning of 2002 that would change my life forever. At a New Year's Eve party in Hackney, I, among other partygoers, witnessed the murder of two men. A single shot was fired. The bullet went through one man, ricocheted against the wall and entered the head of a second man. The following day I found out that the second man was my friend's brother.

For months after I was disturbed by the death of these young men. What had started off as isolated incidents in the commonly recognised black areas, such as Brixton and Hackney, fast became a daily occurrence of random shootings. I became insanely frightened for my brothers. In July that year my fears were realised, with the murder of my eighteen year old brother. Gun crime had now become my own reality. I joined the chorus of lament for the deaths of sons, brothers, fathers and lovers. But I also wanted to understand what was happening and why. Commentary in the media has tended to be sensational scare mongering; often with barely concealed racial overtones. What sympathetic coverage there has been - a few TV documentaries and broadsheet features - has failed to develop an analysis which puts the phenomenon of young black men killing other young black men into a wider political and economic context.

The accelerating occurrences of gun crime in Lambeth, Brent and Hackney have resulted in a slew of community, police and government partnership programmes. However, because there is no centralised system that can measure or assess their performance, it is difficult to discern their true impact. The young people I spoke with did not cite any of the plethora of anti-gun crime initiatives as a factor in diverting them from crime. In fact, their overwhelming belief was that gun crime was inevitable. While I do not wish to discount the significant and necessary work of anti-gun crime programmes, the question of their effectiveness needs to be addressed - and I hope that it will be in the forthcoming Metropolitan Police Authority's Gun Crime Scrutiny Review.

Having said that, it has been a significant development that the establishment has recognised that the social and economic condition of inner city children in general, and black children in particular, is a major factor leading them to engage in crime. It has led to proactive work aiming to redress the social and economic imbalance through education, training and employment. These are areas which have previously failed disaffected black people. However, in my own personal experience, disaffection does not apply to all black people from impoverished backgrounds. Many young black people have transcended social and economic deprivation and there is much to be learned from how they have achieved this. For example, what can we learn from black girls' positive attitude towards education (although not necessarily toward school)?

I want to make a start on developing an understanding of gun crime by first giving a voice to those at the centre of the problem - black young men and women - and seeing what they might be able to tell us. All the extracts which follow are taken from discussions with people from the south London borough of Lambeth, which is one of the Metropolitan Police's Operation Trident 'hotspots'.

I ask Robert who is sixteen what it was like growing up in Brixton.

Robert   Hard. Say we're going out, we can't go nowhere without police following behind us or just stopping us on the road.

Ejos   From what age did you start experiencing that?

Robert   Nine, ten. The way I used to go on on road was not like a bad boy, but we were young, so we just carried on how kids would act. But they'd just think 'they're bad boys, they've probably got drugs or guns on them'. So they'd just pull us over and stop us.

Shareen and Nadia, both young women, aged 18 and 14, describe a gun culture they perceive as widespread.

Shareen and Nadia   You know, gun crime has risen to the point where everybody on the street these days have a gun. Boys as young as 12 are carrying guns. That's what people do.

Ejos   We say it so naturally but that's not what everybody does. Who are we talking about?

Shareen and Nadia Friends, family, people we know. Either they've got a gun, they know someone that's got a gun or they're involved in a gun crime.

Ejos Is it just for protection or is it for stripes?

Shareen Yeah it is for protection, but it's also for, 'yeah I'm a bad boy I carry a gun'.

Ejos Black men, or men in general involved in street culture, feel that they have to take on that 'I'm not afraid of anyone' persona.

Shareen Otherwise you get taken for a boy - and when I say taken for a boy, people take the piss if you don't react the way they want you to react. They will take you for a boy, that's how they see it.

Nadia If you ain't got money you're a prick.

Shareen Then you can't get a girl, because you can't buy her things, and you can't purchase things to make you look good, to even get a girl.

Kane was convicted and imprisoned for a firearm offence. He illuminates the complexities that black males face in our society.

Kane I tell you what, money goes to your head, and with a gun on top of that you start getting that extra power. Money, power, respect. You can gain respect from people if you've got money. I'm not saying every man's got to be that way. That doesn't make you a man. But the man I want to be, that's what it is.

Kane echoes the sentiments of all the young people I spoke with. For them money is the only tangible marker of success, and as disenfranchised black people, particularly black men, they can rarely access this through legitimate work. They seek other alternatives, mainly through 'hustling'.

Kane I grew up on an estate and the role models are the people that are doing well for themselves, because everyone's living in, you could say, poverty. So, you look to who's ever looking good, who's ever making life looking interesting. When you get to the stage where the usual stuff boys do is getting boring now, you either want girls or money, or both. I was more like I was going to get money. I saw the older guys and they were doing their thing. And that's who are your role models when you're on an estate.

Ejos Would you say you were poor?

Kane I wouldn't say I was, but what I say to my mum when she say's she tried the best for us is, at the end of the day we live in an estate and you've got to face that everyday, so you've got to be a certain way to survive. So if you did so well for us why we still living here? If my dad was a successful person I wouldn't be living on an estate, would I? We'd be living in a nice house, going to a private school and all that stuff. But obviously that didn't happen. So to me he's not the best role model, because he hasn't got what I consider to be the qualities of life.

Ejos What are the qualities of life?

Kane When I see people that have had a good education, and the way they look at life and the things they get up to, it looks a lot - I don't know - *easier* for them. Their parents are always willing to help them out, through Uni and stuff. We didn't have all that stuff so we'll always look for an alternative.

Ejos What's the alternative?

Kane I suppose you want the fast money now. You don't want to go the long way. I think it is much more of a struggle for someone who hasn't got a rich father to go through Uni. And when you're going back and forth to Uni every day, you come home and see this guy down the road who seems to have everything that you want and you're trying to strive for. It depends what you want. I'm talking more material things, but then I suppose I'm more materialistic because I've seen what material things can do.

Respect and conflict

The culture of respect plays an important part in escalating conflict between young men. To try and make sense of it I am speaking with James who is 16, and Trevor who is an older man and his mentor. James was born in Jamaica and came to England in his early teens. He offers a unique transcultural perspective of gun culture from his first-hand experience of gun crime, which begins in his early years in Jamaica and continues when he migrates to England. Our conversation takes place in Trevor's car as we drive across South London.

Ejos   How much did your gun cost you to get?

James   My dad gave it to me.

Ejos   So you were how old?

James   About 12.

Ejos   Have you ever shot after anybody?

James   Yeah.

Ejos   Have you been shot?

James   Yeah I've been grazed.

Ejos   I'd be shook if I thought somebody was trying to kill me.

James   I never cared whether I died or not.

Ejos   Why is that?

James   That was just my mentality then!

Ejos   You didn't value your life?

James Nope.

Ejos Did you enjoy your life?

James Yeah.

Ejos So the thought of you being taken away from that life didn't really matter?

James I never had that thought.

Ejos Were you in a crew? How many of you were there?

James 30. I built the crew.

Ejos So did that make you the top boy?

James Nah, it never made me the top boy, I was just like anyone else.

Ejos What did you do?

James Everything like bad boys, like rude kids do, like going out beating people up, shooting after people, running up on people, all of that. Just for fun - nothing better to do.

Ejos Was there money involved?

James At first when we started it was just for fun, until some of us realised what we could get out of doing it, so we just started doing it on the regs, on the regular.

Ejos Is it from street robberies to jacking people?

James Street robberies, big robberies like running up on shotters [drug dealers, usually class A drugs] and stuff like that.

Ejos So, running up on shotters your age?

James Nah, shotters all ages. Big man like, big guys in the business. I ran up on man and take his ting - they're boys.

Ejos For me, if you're gonna run up on certain man they're looking to dead you. There are just certain man you can't - I don't know, you tell me.

James You can run up on anyone, you just have to know what you're doing.

Ejos Did it ever get to a point where people suspected you?

James Yeah, that's why we had to shoot after people. We had to stand our ground because they suspected it was us, because it was only us that had the crew, so they figured it out.

Ejos You make it sound quite organised. It's the same kind of thinking you apply to setting up your own business - getting the staff together, having your daily objectives. Did you plan it?

James Yeah we did.

Ejos What would you do with the money?

James Buy whatever I wanted, buy trainers, buy clothes. I'd squander my money.

Ejos What made you change?

James I was getting older, and the more older the more dangerous, the more things that would happen, so I just left it, cut that game.

While we're talking a group of young boys in school uniform are fighting on road corner. They capture our attention.

Trevor They're playing about.

Ejos No they're not! They're battering the shit out of him. Is that how boys play about?

James They're play fighting.

Trevor They're not doing nothing but play fighting.

Ejos Ok, but that kind of play gets serious.

Trevor I know that. I don't play with friends like that, me na ramp wid people at all. Exactly it just get serious and people think they know your strength because maybe they've handled you a little way. Before you know it they wanna try and bully you now, because they think they're stronger than you. So I don't play none of that. But they're youngsters, so they have to live and learn.

Ejos I was going to ask you what your relationship is like with the men in your family?

James My relationship with my whole family is cool.

Ejos How does your mum feel about your lifestyle?

James Obviously she don't like it. No mum would like that. She can probably see some of the places it's coming from. She keeps asking me why do I do it. I can't tell her why I do it. I used to do it for the fun of it, just for the excitement - and for the reputation, obviously, because you get a reputation from doing it. I had my reputation before I started doing it because the way my mentality was - I don't care, I could die any day, so not anyone could say anything to me and I would just flip. But now I look at it differently. That's how I got stabbed in my face twice in two months.

Ejos What was that over?

James One was over a girl, a next one was over my brethren popping a chain - just a madness.

Ejos When you say it's over a girl I just find that interesting, because there's no men fighting over me - not that I would want them to. So I just want to know what's going on?

James His girl must have slept over at my house and my girl found out, and told her brethren. Her brethren text her and told her that was a violation, because her brethren thought I slept with her. The youth's brethren saw the text in my girl's phone, went back to his brethren and told him I fucked his girl. He came on the hype.

Ejos What are you going to do?

James What am I going to do to him?

Trevor He ain't doing nothing.

James I ain't doing nothing man.

Ejos So where has that change in mentality come from? I can imagine that five years ago you would have wanted to kill him straight?

James I would've dead him. Once he had shank [stabbed] me, I wouldn't have dead him, my boys would have done it. But I told them to allow it, because when he did it people had straps [guns] on them, and they were like 'here, here, do that', and I was ... we just had a little madness. I never knew he shank me because it was a bang. I never knew he shank me till after. One day I caught him and I was gonna burst him, but, true say, it was in Brixton and I left it.

Ejos Why, is Brixton hot?

James Yeah, Brixton's hot, there's cameras in Brixton. There was too much people there. I just left him. He called me and said, 'Why are we beefing?'

Ejos I think ultimately he's shooked, because he's phoned you and apologised. So in essence, if it's a winning, don't you think you've won?

James Yeah basically.

Ejos So why the need to scuff?

James He bust my lip! No one can bust my lip, that's my face. With someone else it would've been a minor, but that's my face.

Ejos From what I hear, you saying you come from a family that's got a rep. When you were growing up did you feel that pressure?

James Nah, I never felt that pressure because I never needed to. Once they knew my family background it was like, 'nah I'm not touching that kid!'

Ejos So is it like you said, you just wanted to do it?

James I just wanted to do it.

Ejos It's about power. You didn't use that word, but I've come to that understanding from reading theorists and the ideas of people. Often with men in general, and black men in particular because of the way society is structured, from when you're young you're socialised to believe that it's natural for boys to fight. We accept that's how boys are raised.

Trevor Don't cry, be hard. You're always telling your boy child, 'Don't cry, be hard!' You arm the young boys with the skills for them to survive within the society. I've got a son, I've got a daughter, and it's the same thing, they don't grow the same. My son gets armoured with the skills, so a lot of the things that my daughter might brush off my son can't brush off, get used to, because it's a hard world. So, yeah, from a young age boys are given, this - not violence tendency, but they're given this hard exterior. Society demands it.

Ejos Well I understand that from my brothers' experiences. With my older brother, he built a reputation on the streets, so by the time he first went inside his reputation was solid in West [West London], and I later learned that he was known in other areas as a kind of street legend. When he went inside my four remaining brothers were 14, 15 and two of them 13. My parents took the two older ones to Nigeria because they saw what was coming, leaving the two 13 year olds behind because they thought they were still young. But as one of them was coming up he felt the pressure and he went about establishing his own rep.

The reason why we started this conversation was because of power. Within this society black men don't have that 'real' power that they seek. Most men are socialised to seek power, in the belief that power validates their manhood. It's how much money you have, if you can provide for your family.

James   It depends the power that you want. You can have power of running the streets, you can have power of running your family, you can have power of running the whole world.

Ejos   Ultimately, the power I'm speaking about is to be able to provide for yourself and provide for your family.

James   That's what makes you man, when you can provide for your family.

Trevor   A man is a man who can defend what is his, which includes his family and anything that belongs to him. I tell you, that is what the youth really want. When you hear them talking about power - maybe he can't explain himself properly or maybe he ain't breaking it down - but I've seen with young people especially, what means the most to them is that power, not self respect but people respecting them. So that's the most powerful thing to a young person. A lot of them don't make a dime. Money! They don't ever make money. Money! What do they know about money? They make chump change. To them, as far as they're concerned, if someone's stepping to them and invading their space and disrespecting them, they're willing to kill over that. They don't kill over their family, a lot of them don't care about their family, because if they did they wouldn't put their mum through a lot, and their brothers and sisters in harm's reach - because a lot of the time, when they're in beef it's their brothers and sisters who get it. So to me they are totally misguided in their principles, or what they say is important to them, and that's a fact!

Ejos   James what's your response to that?

Trevor   It's a macho thing.

James   That's the mentality of everyone. Once they know you've got a gun they won't want to step to you. Once you've got a gun and anyone steps to you, you're gonna use it. That's the advantage you've got.

Trevor   That's the disadvantage to it!

James   It's a disadvantage as well.

Trevor   That every time you have an argument you're gonna use it.

Ejos   James believes it's an advantage because it affords him power. Trevor sees it as a disadvantage because he knows that ultimately you're gonna end up dead or in prison.

Trevor   Definitely. I've been there, done it. Everything James is going done, I've done it a million times over. I'm 38. I've spent seven and a half years of my life in prison. There ain't no crime I haven't committed or been involved in. I've lived in Brixton all my life, so what these young people go through, for me, unless there's an ulterior motive that's productive - we're talking about making money and investing it into a legitimate business and getting yourself out of the game - as far as I'm concerned, they've lost the plot totally. Young people nowadays, you heard James say it as well, he squandered money.

Ejos   James you're very articulate, I have to say that, but I don't expect any less anyway. Once I was speaking with my brother and he was trying to school me on cultural books. I was like, 'Listen mate I've read those books'. But I was surprised because he was reading books that I was reading at university. He was reading them because he was interested in them - so I'm not surprised. I say this all the time, the same drive that you lot apply on road is the same drive that you must and can apply to do something positive.

James That's why I've cut my road life earlier than some people have. The earlier you cut your road life the better it is, you have more opportunity. For some people there's an end. For some there's not. Some people do it because they have to do it, some people do it for the reputation and just for the fun of doing it. You've got some people, when they fire guns, the way they love firing guns, they'll keep on firing it and firing it, and they'll either end up dead, in prison, or they'll kill bare [lots of] people. I always say this to people. It's not about what you do and what comes straight after, it's the consequences you pay after what you've done that hurts most. Because if you've killed someone, you've got to live with your conscience for the rest of your life - that, rah, I've taken that person's life and any day someone can know that it's you, and someone else just run up on you and take yours. Then where's that gonna leave your family? Even though you done already mash up one family, your family's gonna get mashed up. You could have your own kids and that, their Dad get killed, and if your kids are big they're going to want to retaliate. Everyone makes their choices, everyone's got a choice in life. If you want to follow the road life, you can follow the road life. If you want to go straight, you can go straight. I've seen it. There's 'nough of my brethrens dem that I wish I'd followed when I was younger. But I can't turn back the hands of time. So all I have to do now is try to change from now for the future, because I can't change the past. What I did I've done. I can't go back and say I'm going to give back that person all the money that he gave to me, because I don't know how much money he gave to me, that's how mad it is. I have been through so much things and seen so much things, I've seen 'nough people get killed, I've seen people getting killed and shitting themselves as they're dying. I've seen all that. I've been in shoot outs with man. It's what the consequences are, because if someone was to shoot me and my people know who it is, I know that person's gonna die if they catch him. But the way how my life is, there is so much enemies that I've got, if someone was to kill me no one would know who it is, but yet still someone else would die for it - even if it's not them, someone will die.

Ejos If you were to die would you want your people to retaliate?

James I can't really say because I don't really know my view on that right about now. Obviously I'm not matured enough like you lot are, but from my point of view, yeah, I would want someone to die back for it. But maybe if I was a bit older and understanding life a bit more, probably no I wouldn't. I'd have the same views as you. But because of how young I am, obviously my view's going to be different from yours.

Ejos   Where do you see yourself in five years?

James   In five years I want to be playing football, that's what I want to be doing, but I can't definitely say that I will be playing football. Obviously my dream is to play for Manchester United. I want to but I'm not going to say I will make it, because the way how life is, it might not turn out the way I want to.

We're back in James's neighbourhood and, as Trevor is about to drop James off, there are a group of young men standing on the corner of the road. James informs us that he is in conflict with them, so Trevor continues driving. James immediately becomes defensive, assuming a hyper-masculine posturing.

Trevor   Do you want to be dropped somewhere else? I'm not dropping you here.

James   Why not? They've seen me!

Conclusion

In 2005 gun crime rose by more than 50 per cent despite huge efforts by Trident and the black community to combat it. And as it has risen so has the number of black males imprisoned for these offences. There is now an alarming number of young black men facing life imprisonment. I am not suggesting that these men should not be made accountable for their crimes. But the judicial system pathologises black males, and rarely ever gives serious consideration to the impact of their social and material condition. There is a fundamental need for long-term solutions that will alleviate the social and economic conditions that lie at the root of gun crime. In the meantime the most effective kinds of intervention are those in which the lived experience of the young men is understood and embraced. Black men, particularly those from the streets, and who most likely have a criminal experience, are pivotal in influencing the hard-to-reach young people. Both James and Robert cite Trevor as a major influence in diverting them away from crime.

But alongside economic change and community intervention, we need to challenge patriarchal ideas of masculinity. All the young men concurred that men are socialised to accept violence as a norm. Kane explains: 'In our culture we seem to accept violence as a way of disputing things, to argue things out'. Explaining why he carried a gun, he says:

> I'm not the instigator. I've got no reason for that, I'm a business man, it don't make no sense. But you've got to try and protect the investment. If someone's trying to do you something, you've got to be able to defend yourself, and there's no point putting out fists these days, because that's not gonna get you nowhere.

And with the gun comes power:

> But one thing is, when you start, it brings a sense of power, and when the power comes you feel the man. No one can fuck with you, you feel invincible.

Kane realised that street crime only gave him false power, limited to the streets. But instead of adopting a more consciously critical position, he now seeks affirmation of his manhood through material wealth. He is playing the capitalist game, pursuing the same power that the white middle class have. In his attempts to counter the stereotypes of black male identity he has ended up adopting an ideal of success not very different from the Thatcherite individualism of the 1980s.

Men who, refusing to be victims of a hierarchical political economy, have sought alternative means of economic production to provide for themselves and their families, have done so at the price of losing their souls, and their lives. Kane expresses the pain and crisis that black males face in their struggle to be self-determining:

Ejos Were you not afraid when the gun was being pointed at you?

Kane No, I weren't afraid of none of that, truthfully.

Ejos How does it happen - you just don't think about it?

Kane You know what it goes back to ... I never really felt love, in a sense of - I don't know, how can I explain it - inside, deep down, nothing really bothered me. I can't really explain it. It's just a feeling within ... I feel, when you hold it deep inside, it just makes you want to give out pain. You don't really care about other people because you might be going through things yourself that are making you feel pain, and you feel no-one cares about you. When you've got that sort of anger inside you, it will make you easily not care about others.

Ejos Do you think you had a lack of respect for life?

Kane Definitely - if you have all that anger inside, you act on instinct rather than think things through.

If we are to alleviate gun crime, we must do the brave and radical work of interrogating patriarchal masculinity and a culture of domination - as well as advocating new avenues for self-actualisation that foster the emotional well being of disaffected black people. Just as many women have found agency in the therapeutic discourse of dialogue, so can men.

In loving memory of Junior

A new politics of respect

Ruth Lister

Ruth Lister argues that it is central to the agenda of anti-poverty politics to give recognition, respect and voice to those living in poverty.

If you put me in chains,
then hatred reigns,
and fear gains control of you.
I will not come as a prisoner,
I will not come broken to you,
I will come with pride,
and stand by your side,
because I am human too.[1]

This is an extract from a poem written in a creative writing project involving people living in poverty. Its eloquence about the experience of poverty goes beyond statistics. Poverty is experienced not only as a wretched and insecure economic condition, but also as a shameful and destructive social relation. This article addresses both these dimensions, with particular attention to the latter, and argues for recognition of the agency, human rights and common citizenship of people living in poverty.

Existing not living

When people on low incomes are asked to describe their lives the common refrain is that they are 'existing not living'. Whatever the consequences and

---

1. Anonymous, reproduced from Liz Prest (ed), *Out of the Shadows*, 2000, with the kind permission of ATD Fourth World. For more poems, see pp99-100.

conditions associated with poverty, an inadequate income and material hardship are at its heart.[2] This is what differentiates the state of poverty from non-poverty. Going without, constrained choices leaving little room for spontaneity, running out of money, debt - all of these are typical of the living conditions of people on low benefits and wages. To be poor is to live a life of insecurity and vulnerability, in which the delicate balancing act of getting by can be upset by minor breakdowns of equipment or losses that the rest of us can take in our stride, cushioned as we are by savings or insurance.

P overty in an affluent society spells exclusion from full participation, and this exclusion can be particularly painful for children unable to enjoy the wide range of goods and activities seen as a normal part of childhood today.[3] Marketing and the tyranny of the right brand label create a glass barrier between children in low-income families and the consumer society. The children can see and desire the consumer goods on the other side; and from the other side they are seen as lacking these requisites, especially the right trainers and clothes, which means that they then sometimes suffer further exclusion and even bullying.[4]

In turn, parents - notably mothers, who take the main responsibility for managing poverty, often acting as shock-absorbers as they try to protect other family members from its full impact - feel a sense of failure and guilt. The resulting stress can be damaging to their physical and mental health. As one mother put it, 'poverty ... sucks you in and breaks you'.[5] Richard Wilkinson's recent work demonstrates the psycho-social links between poverty and ill health, and the destructive effects of the glass barrier: 'second-rate goods seem to tell people you are a second-rate person. To believe otherwise is to fundamentally misunderstand the pain of relative poverty or low social status'.[6]

Unfortunately, many do misunderstand that pain. In a recent deliberative qualitative study carried out by MORI for the Fabian Commission on Life

---

2. The article does not address the causes of poverty. These lie in economic, social and political structures and processes. They are manifested in conditions such as low pay, unemployment, lone parenthood, disability and old age.
3. Rowan Williams criticised as unjust marketing aimed at children in *Soundings* 31.
4. See Tess Ridge, *Childhood Poverty and Social Exclusion*, Policy Press, 2002; and Ed Mayo, *Shopping Generation*, National Consumer Council, 2005.
5. See Women's Budget Group, *Women's and Children's Poverty: making the links*, 2005.
6. Richard Wilkinson, *The Impact of Inequality*, Routledge 2005, p71.

Chances and Child Poverty, participants who were moved by the evidence that lack of money denied children monthly swimming or a birthday celebration remained dismissive of the idea that the inability to afford the latest trainers spells poverty.[7] We need to find ways of encouraging the general public to think about what constitutes a decent and flourishing childhood, and then demonstrate how poverty denies children so many of its basic building blocks. And we need to demonstrate the pain that poverty can cause in a consumer society.

Othering 'the poor'

That pain is psychological. It derives from everyday social relations, and from the ways in which people in poverty are talked about and treated by politicians, officials, professionals, the media and other influential bodies and individuals. According to ATD Fourth World, who work with families in severe and long-term poverty, what makes poverty so hard to bear is 'to know that you count for nothing, to the point where even your suffering is ignored … The worst blow of all is the contempt of your fellow citizens'. (For more information on ATD Fourth World and other anti-poverty organisations mentioned in this article, see websites listed at the end.)

This contempt is one manifestation of a process of Othering: people in poverty are thought about, talked about and treated as 'Other' to the rest of society. Through this process of differentiation and demarcation, social distance is established and maintained. The dividing line is imbued with negative judgements that construct 'the poor' variously as a source of moral contamination, a threat, an undeserving economic burden, an object of pity or even as an exotic species. It affirms 'our' identity and legitimates our privilege while denying 'them' their complex humanity and subjectivity. In doing so, it all too easily serves to justify poverty and inequality by blaming the 'Other' for their own and also society's problems. An example is provided by the initial stance adopted by participants in the MORI/Fabian study. They demonstrated a deep lack of empathy with people living in poverty, who were seen as different - to the extent that when participants did acknowledge the existence of child poverty they tended to blame it on parental behaviour.

---

7. *Why Life Chances Matter*, interim report, Fabian Society 2005.

'Othering' can be understood in part as a discursive practice. It shapes how those without experience of poverty think and talk about and act towards those living in poverty, at both an inter-personal and an institutional level. The language and labels used to describe 'the poor' have been articulated by the more powerful 'non-poor', and are often rooted in history. The most obviously demeaning examples are the labels of 'underclass' and 'welfare dependant'.

However, the less value-laden term 'poor' is also a problem. When it is used as a noun - 'the poor'- it lumps together disparate groups and individuals as if this were their one defining characteristic. (I do so here only in quotation marks to denote the term's problematic status.) Used as an adjective, 'poor' can carry connotations of inferior, as in 'poor quality'. Either way, people who are labelled with these words can be bitterly resentful of what they perceive to be stigmatising descriptions of themselves - and of the neighbourhoods in which they live. This has implications for collective identity and agency: 'proud to be poor' is not a banner under which many want to march.

These difficulties also raise questions for commentators and campaigners: if, in deference to the understandable sensibilities of those concerned, we avoid all reference to poverty in favour of terms such as 'low income' (as did the Thatcher government for very different reasons), it can weaken the moral impetus to act. The pragmatic compromise adopted by some campaigners is to talk about 'people with experience of poverty' or 'living in poverty'. This denotes a more respectful stance, which does not assume poverty to be a defining characteristic, but treats it as a socio-economic condition, and one in which far too many people are living. Nor does the term 'social exclusion' solve the dilemma. Not many to whom the label is customarily attached have heard of the term, and there has been no research on how it is perceived by those to whom it refers. There is some disagreement among commentators as to whether or not it avoids the derogatory overtones of existing labels. This is partly because it is deployed politically within a number of competing discourses, which have very different implications for those it describes and for policies towards them.

One of the ways in which political language constructs 'the poor' and 'socially excluded' is by virtue of contrasting discourses. Most notable at present is the New Labour mantra of 'hard-working families', implicitly - or sometimes explicitly - prefaced with 'decent'. Since it is generally assumed that people in poverty do not work hard, 'hard working families readily becomes a counterpart to negative stereotypes of lazy, non-working poor families', as the Fabian Commission noted (p50).

The Othering of 'the poor' is reinforced by media representations, which may be the main source of information about poverty for much of the rest of the population, especially now that wealth and disadvantage have become more spatially polarised. Research has illuminated some of the ways in which media images confirm negative stereotypes and contribute to the development of punitive attitudes towards recipients of benefit. This can be the effect of even sympathetic accounts. An example of this sympathetic Othering can be found in the widely publicised *Dark Heart: the Shocking Truth about Hidden Britain*, by the campaigning journalist, Nick Davies (Vintage 1998). Davies presents himself as 'a Victorian explorer penetrating a distant jungle', 'another' 'undiscovered country'. He frequently uses the adjective 'different' to underline the message. This means the book is more likely to distance its readers and instil fear than to inspire a 'crusade against poverty' as Davies had hoped. The MORI/Fabian research suggested that images that appeal to pity also create distance and encourage a perception of those in poverty as other.

People in poverty are themselves consumers of the media of course. They see and hear the stigmatising images and language. As a parent on benefit told the All-Parliamentary Group on Poverty, 'we hear how the media, and some politicians, speak about us and it hurts'. More generally, the Othering of people in poverty means that they are frequently targets of pity or indifference - and sometimes fear, contempt and hostility. As a consequence people in poverty often feel humiliated. The effects of this can be injurious to identity, self-respect and self-esteem. An anonymous participant in a UK Coalition Against Poverty (UKCAP) workshop described what this can feel like: 'You're like an onion and gradually every skin is peeled off you and there's nothing left. All your self-esteem and how you feel about yourself is gone - you're left feeling like nothing and then your family feels like that'.

Reactions to stigmatising Othering vary. When it is internalised, as vividly expressed in the onion metaphor, shame is a likely consequence. In a visit to the UK, two community workers from south India remarked on the degree of stigma, and associated sense of shame, that they observed among people living in poverty. An alternative response is anger, as witnessed recently in France, when Interior Minister Nicolas Sarkozy's use of the term 'racaille' (translated variously as 'rabble' and 'scum') inflamed the anger already felt by young people in the banlieues. Sarkozy aggravated their sense of exclusion - which derives from the all too common compound of poverty and racial discrimination.

An alternative language: human rights and citizenship

'Othering' - whether hostile, indifferent or sympathetic - treats people living in poverty as objects. In contrast, and also as a response, participatory research and action against poverty acknowledges people's subjectivity and agency; this includes both the agency involved in getting by in constrained circumstances, and the political agency necessary for citizenship. Participatory approaches are increasingly informed by an alternative set of discourses, ones that demand dignifying treatment and respect for people who are fellow human beings and citizens. As Millicent Simms, a young unemployed woman, told a UK National Poverty Hearing (organised by Church Action on Poverty): 'You shouldn't have to be made to feel as though you are useless. I just feel very angry sometimes that people are ignorant to the fact that we are humans as well and we do need to be respected'. Her anger was reflected in much of the evidence received by the Commission on Poverty, Participation and Power (commissioned by UKCAP in 1999), who reported that 'the lack of respect for people living in poverty was one of the clearest and most heartfelt messages which came across to us as a Commission'.[8]

This is the flipside of Tony Blair's respect agenda - which tends to ignore the reciprocal nature of respect and the power relations underpinning it (though the Social Exclusion Unit has recently acknowledged lack of respect as a significant issue for disadvantaged groups). The importance of respectful treatment to people living in poverty is underlined in Richard Sennett's argument: 'lack of respect, though less aggressive than outright insult, can take an equally wounding form. No insult is offered another person, but neither is recognition extended; he or she is not *seen* ... as a full human being whose

---

8. Commission on Poverty, Participation and Power, *Listen Hear: The right to be heard*, Policy Press 2000, p3.

presence matters'.[9] An informant in one study described himself as 'stigmatised through mental health problems, unemployment, poverty and other means of social exclusion' and as 'a zero'. As he explained, that 'nothing at all' value is 'a destroying experience ... I am invisible'.[10]

Philosophers such as John Rawls and Martha Nussbaum identify self-respect as critical to human functioning. Nussbaum makes clear the link between self-respect and dignifying treatment by others, rooted in recognition of equal worth. But, as a mother in a study I was involved in told us: 'poverty strips your dignity. You can't have any dignity with poverty'.[11] This is all the more the case in a society where the better-off are so far socially removed from those living in poverty that they are incapable of recognising the latter as dignified beings who are their equals.

Dignity is at the heart of conceptualisations of poverty based on human rights and citizenship. And such conceptualisations are key elements in an alternative poverty discourse that is emerging in both the global North and South. This discourse seeks to combat the process of Othering; it recognises the humanity and agency of people in poverty and connects with wider political and democratic struggles. And it may offer a language that can help to inspire a domestic campaign rooted in solidarity between non-poor and poor.

The UN has been instrumental in promoting a human rights conceptualisation of poverty. Across Europe, the language of human rights underpins the anti-poverty and social exclusion strategy propounded by the European Anti-Poverty Network (EAPN). In the US, people in poverty and homeless people have come together in the Poor People's Economic Human Rights Campaign 'to raise the issue of poverty as a human rights violation'. They have conducted a number of national economic human rights marches. The language of human rights, drawing on the civil rights movement, is being used to counter the negative associations typically provoked by the image of 'poor'. However, while this offers a valuable mobilising tool, the MORI/Fabian study suggests that it needs to be used with care. For some participants, the language of human rights conjured up images of poverty in the

9.   Richard Sennett, *Respect*, Allen Lane 2003, p3, emphasis in original.
10. S. J. Charlesworth, 'Understanding social suffering', *Journal of Community & Applied Social Psychology*, 15, 2005, pp304-5.
11. Peter Beresford *et al*, *Poverty First Hand*, Child Poverty Action Group, 1999, p90.

global South; only after they had been confronted with stark statistics on unequal life chances, such as those showing reduced life expectancy, did they come to see a human rights framework as relevant.

Within the context of individual nation states, human rights translate into more concrete citizenship rights. At the first European meeting of Citizens Living in Poverty participants stressed that they wanted to be seen first and foremost as citizens before they were categorised as people living in poverty (for more on this meeting, see EAPN website). For them this meant staking a common claim and being part of society's mainstream, able to participate fully in the social, economic, political, civic and cultural spheres. Participation in the political sphere and in decision-making is a particularly significant aspect of citizenship in the civic republican tradition. In the context of poverty, a UN practice note states that:

> the notion of participation is at the centre of a human rights-based approach to poverty reduction. The poor … can no longer be seen as passive recipients; they are strategic partners rather than target groups. Human rights change in a fundamental way the relationship between service providers and service recipients.

Participation is a crucial human and citizenship right because it explicitly acknowledges the agency of rights-bearers, as the UN statement underlines. It also underpins the effective realisation of other rights. It directly addresses the issues of voicelessness and powerlessness that are frequently identified as critical by people in poverty. Calls for the voices of the marginalised to be heard in policy-making and campaigning are becoming more pressing. And these calls also draw on principles of social inclusion and democracy. They represent a demand for recognition of, and respect for, the expertise borne of experience, as exemplified by the poems reproduced at the end of this article. As Moraene Roberts, an activist with ATD Fourth World, told the national poverty hearing mentioned earlier: 'No-one asks our views … But we are the real experts of our own hopes and aspirations … We can contribute if you are prepared to give up a little power to allow us to participate as partners in our own future'.

Enabling the voices of people with experience of poverty to be heard is one way of counteracting the lack of recognition and respect accorded them.

It is a way of seeing - and hearing - people in poverty as human beings whose presence matters. Voicelessness is also associated with powerlessness: it is symptomatic of the political powerlessness of people in poverty, as well as a cause of their feelings of powerlessness. 'Power not pity' is one of the demands of the US Poor People's Economic Human Rights Campaign. However voice alone, though necessary, is not enough: in the words of John Gaventa of the Institute for Development Studies, it needs to be 'voice with influence'. One of the clearest messages received by the Commission on Poverty, Participation and Power was that 'people experiencing poverty see consultation without commitment, and phoney participation without the power to bring about change, as the ultimate disrespect' (p18, see note 7).

A politics of recognition&respect

The growing demands of poverty activists for recognition of their human rights, citizenship and voice suggest that the politics of poverty needs to be framed not just as a politics of redistribution - important as that still is - but also as a politics of recognition; or, to reflect the language used by people in poverty themselves, a politics of recognition&respect. I am drawing here on the work of political theorists such as Nancy Fraser and Axel Honneth. Although their writings on social justice tend not to address poverty as such, they offer a framework for recasting the politics of poverty. The politics of recognition is typically associated with the assertion of group difference and identity, for example by women, lesbians and gays and racialised groups. However, the last thing that people in poverty want is to be treated as different. Instead, their demand is for recognition of their common humanity and citizenship and the equal worth and respect that flows from that.

Recognition politics also requires us to acknowledge the psychological pain and suffering that poverty can inflict. The author of an insightful study of Australian poverty quoted the people living in poverty to whom he spoke as making it clear that 'if social justice is a response to poverty … it must be a response to poverty's psychological and emotional wounds, not just its financial consequences'. He quotes one of the people he spoke to: 'You can put up with the struggle, you know, just get by, if you get respect and if you're treated right'.[12]

---

12. Mark Peel, *The Lowest Rung*, Cambridge University Press 2003, p167.

A combined politics of redistribution and recognition&respect would aim both to eradicate poverty and thereby remove the need to struggle to 'get by', and to ensure that those who nevertheless remain in poverty 'get respect' and 'are treated right'. It reinforces the case for adequate benefits and wages, which must be at a level consistent with human dignity as well as sufficient to meet needs. It points to the need to foster 'poverty-awareness' among all those involved in developing and delivering services that affect people living in poverty, for instance by involving the service-users in policy-development and in the training of professionals.[13]

P overty politics must combat the process of Othering through the involvement of people in poverty as political citizens. It also needs to combat the tendency to residualise the issue of poverty by embedding it into other political debates such as those about democracy, well-being and inequalities. The continued existence of such high levels of poverty is an affront to democracy and is incompatible with the kind of flourishing and just society to which the democratic left aspires.

The article draws on my book Poverty, *Polity Press 2004.*

Websites of organisations mentioned in the text
ATD Fourth World: www.atd-uk.org
UK Coalition Against Poverty: www.ukcap.org
European Anti-Poverty network: www.eapn.org/code/en/hp.asp
Church Action on Poverty: www.church-poverty.org.uk

---

13. For example, ATD Fourth World, the Family Rights Group and Royal Holloway have developed a training module on poverty for social work students to be delivered by people with experience of poverty. In Belgium, 'experiential experts', with experience of poverty, are being trained to act as mediators within government agencies.

Living on nothing

Living on nothing is trying not to see the
wretchedness and the despair,
living on nothing is trying not to feel the loss of hope.

Living on nothing is trying not to taste the
anger and the disappointment.
Living on nothing is trying not to smell the fear.

Living on nothing is trying not to hear the intellectual
arguments and lofty ideals about
living on nothing put forward by those who
are not living on nothing.
Living on nothing is dying.

All people, all human

I'm telling the people with power
that I have power too.
If you stifle my voice,
and deny me a choice,
I will show my power to you.
I will not come with a weapon,
I will not come in fear.
I will come with others
as sisters and brothers
and a voice you will have to hear.

I'm telling the people with knowledge
that I have knowledge too.
If you ignore my words,
and deny what you've heard,
my knowledge will be lost to you.
I will not come in anger,
I will not come in pain,
I will come as me,
with dignity,
and your denial will be to your shame.

I'm telling the people with control,
that I have control too.
If you put me in chains,
then hatred reigns,
and fear gains control of you.
I will not come as a prisoner,
I will not come broken to you,
I will come with pride,
and stand by your side,
because I am human too.

(From *Out of the Shadows*)

Northern Ireland: the problems of identity politics

Robin Wilson

Robin Wilson *argues that it is vital to find new ways of dismantling communalism - and not just in Northern Ireland.*

Another article about Northern Ireland might at first sight seem of no interest to most *Soundings* readers. Yet, amid growing hostility in Britain to asylum-seekers and settled Muslims, and particularly in the fevered atmosphere since the terrorist atrocities of 7 July (in which it seems that even the stark lessons of internment in 1971 can be forgotten), the longstanding challenges of interethnic accommodation in Northern Ireland may perhaps appear of some relevance.

The current approach of the governments in London and Dublin is perhaps not the best place to look for lessons. At the time of writing they were preparing, yet again, for one more heave to restore to the region power-sharing devolution, after its collapse in 2002 amid growing intercommunal polarisation. A range of political sweeteners were being offered to woo into a deal the polarised representatives of intransigence - the now mutually empowered Sinn Féin and Democratic Unionist Party (a deal that Paul Bew has caustically dismissed as an Ulster version of the Molotov-Ribbentrop pact). Any administration resulting from this, even were the two governments to succeed before their latest deadline - May 2007 - would likely represent a sectarian carve-up, rather than a progenitor of reconciliation.

There is no intellectual or moral compass underpinning this approach. This could be seen, for example, in the Northern Ireland Offences Bill's denial of justice to the victims of violence perpetrated by those in and out of uniform since 1968 (this lack of compass is indicative of the broader vacuum at the heart of 'New Labour') - though, thankfully, the bill has been withdrawn. This vacuum then fosters an 'auction mentality' among the protagonists, engendered by those who seek to manage ethnic conflicts by mere *Realpolitik*, thereby stimulating a never-ending politics of grievance.

So is there an alternative left project for interethnic integration - which, in the wake of the riots in the French *banlieues*, must be even more clearly distinguished from assimilation - one that can inform a new course for Northern Ireland, and simultaneously illuminate arguments on the left in Britain about the management of cultural diversity? First, some (much simplified) European left-wing history is in order.

The mission of social-democratic politics

Liberal socialism or social democracy emerged in mass form in the late nineteenth century, with the launch of the Second International on Bastille Day in Paris in 1889 - a hundred years before the fall of the Berlin Wall placed its deformed successor in history's dustbin. While its participants were often enthused by a vulgar-Marxist narrative - in which it was conveniently presumed that a catastrophic crisis of capitalism would issue in the socialist utopia - in practice they operated from day to day according to the pragmatic slogan of the German 'revisionist' Eduard Bernstein: the movement is everything, the goal is nothing. Socialism was not an end in itself but what socialist parties did.[1]

So social democracy sought to tame the capitalist tiger, not to kill it. And to do so it aimed, under progressively more universal franchises, to translate the demographic strength of the emerging working class into a parliamentary majority, capable of introducing reforms which would reduce the exposure of

1. Donald Sassoon, *One Hundred Years of Socialism: The West European Left in the Twentieth Century*, London 1996.

members of that class to the risks of unemployment, poverty, ill-health and so on. Its apogee was the post-war 'welfare states' in western Europe, buttressed by Keynesian demand management, which for the first time allowed (male) full employment and a measure of security against social ills for most working-class people, even if there remained significant numbers of the socially marginalised.

Today, globalisation and individualisation have acted as twin social processes, on a world scale, undermining the sense of the working class as a relatively homogenous social majority, exhibiting a 'natural' solidarity. In the last presidential election in France, for example, the most popular candidate among working-class voters in the first ballot was the neo-fascist Jean-Marie Le Pen.

There is thus no longer any necessary correspondence between social origin and electoral behaviour. Some, though by no means all, members of the older manual working class, retreating into insecurity in today's 'risk society', are vulnerable to conservative and populist - notably anti-immigrant - appeals. Conversely, in a world of mass tertiary education and large-scale public services, some, though by no means all, modern professional workers are amenable to the egalitarian and internationalist appeal of social democracy. If that means that one answer to ethnic division - 'class politics' - is past its sell-by date, it means that another - what I will call a broader 'civic cosmopolitanism' - has much going for it.

Tackling ethnic division: the Austro-Marxists

Actually from the outset social democrats had to face real, often deep, divisions within that supposedly unified working class. As Eric Hobsbawm put it in one of his panoramic lectures on nationalism at Queen's University Belfast twenty years ago: 'from the 1880s on the debate about the "national question" becomes serious and intensive, especially among the socialists, because the political appeal of national slogans to masses of potential or actual voters or supporters of mass political movements was now a matter of real practical concern'.

Nowhere was this debate more developed than among the so-called 'Austro-Marxists', with Otto Bauer and Karl Renner pioneering a way of thinking about ethnic division which avoided the key mistake of reducing it to a plot by the bourgeois parties, instead taking it seriously in its own terms. In the wake of the Russian revolution of 1905, Bauer became concerned about the potential implications for the Habsburg monarchy, and in particular the possibility of worsening relations between German and Czech workers. At the time, a rapidly expanding Vienna had become a multicultural city, with large immigrant populations drawn from a range of nationalities. It was in this context that he wrote *The Question of Nationalities and Social Democracy* in 1906.

The solution Bauer and Renner advanced for coexistence was 'non-territorial national autonomy'. The key distinction is between 'communities of fate' and 'communities of choice':[2] if in the Ottoman empire the millet system essentially assigned people to separate groups, in the Austro-Marxist scheme, as Ephraim Nimni explains in his introduction to Bauer's text, 'the autonomous communities are organized democratically and are based on individual consent to belong and on internal democracy'.[3] This is related to the individualist 'personality principle', which Renner advocated should be formalised as a decision by each citizen as to their nationality upon reaching voting age. Interestingly, this idea originating with the left was able to attract some support from conservatives.

Heinz Fischer, in his foreword to the same book, points to the progressive character of this thinking. Modern social psychology and anthropology would describe it as 'anti-essentialist' (that is to say, recognising that identity cannot be reduced to a single, fixed essence):

> National identities are thus conceptualized in Bauer's study not as 'naturally given' and invariable, but as culturally changeable. Such an understanding would seem to represent a fundamental prerequisite for an approach to national conflicts that operates within a democratic framework and in a spirit of mutual tolerance, rather than in 'biologistic' terms.

This approach was, ironically, too radical for Lenin, who commissioned Stalin to write his wooden *Marxism and the National Question* in response. Stalin adopted instead the inherently collectivist approach of defining the 'nation'

---

2. Paul Hirst, *Associative Democracy: New Forms of Economic and Social Governance*, Cambridge 1994, p49.
3. Otto Bauer, *The Question of Nationalities and Social Democracy*, Minneapolis 2000, pxxvii.

by a set of exactly such taken-for-granted common characteristics (for example language). It was partly for this reason that, after the end of the cold war, 'bureaucratic collectivism' - as the Polish dissidents Kuron and Modzelewski were to describe Soviet-type regimes - could so readily transmute, for some of the nominally leftist parties in power, into ethnic nationalism.

The personality principle, then, would enshrine rights of 'voice' and 'exit' for individuals within the suggested national 'communities'. This remains today an important corrective to what the American leftist Rogers Brubaker calls the 'groupism' that ethno-political entrepreneurs - and some misguided radical advocates of 'identity politics' - are so keen to impose upon the social world.[4] In so far as these groupist political figures succeed, they establish captive clienteles at the expense of the wider social solidarities which socialists are keen to engender.

Despite the significance of the Austro-Marxists' thinking for its time, it was also a product of it. Bauer's attempt to link his theory to his party's official version of Marxism led him to posit a flawed 'national materialism' as a supposed basis for what he called 'national character'. This was derived from an outmoded understanding of evolutionary biology, part Darwinian and part Lamarckian.

In any event, the Habsburg empire collapsed in the furnace of the first world war, when the 'appeal of national slogans' to which Hobsbawm referred was to be all too harshly borne out across Europe, as different 'national' social-democratic parties fell largely in line with 'their' states and the International faced an acute crisis. But the problem was hardly solved by the post-war Versailles formula of 'national self-determination' - which, as Hobsbawm notes, was advanced by Lenin as well as Woodrow Wilson.[5] For this could all too easily translate into a conflict between two equally determined 'selves'.

Instead of addressing the subtle challenge of how individuals of different national affiliations could coexist, as the Austro-Marxists had essayed, the self-determination formula proposed the blunt instrument of 'one people, one state', with all its inevitable consequences for minority oppression, partition and secessionism. As Wilson's secretary of state, an international lawyer called Robert Lansing, prophetically warned: 'The phrase is simply loaded with

4. Rogers Brubaker, 'Ethnicity without groups', *Archives Européenes de Sociologie* 43, 2002.
5. Eric Hobsbawm, *Nations and Nationalism since 1780: Programme, Myth, Reality*, Cambridge 1990.

dynamite … What misery it will cause!' Commitment to this principle was to become the downfall of the inter-war League of Nations, and to offer Hitler a slogan with which he could challenge the Versailles settlement, by raising the plight of the Sudeten Germans who were living in the newly formed state of Czechoslovakia.

As the late Frank Wright put it in his analysis of Northern Ireland: 'Socialism in ethnic frontiers was confronted with a national conflict which no amount of clever theorising or wishful thinking could ever dissipate'. During the partition of Ireland, the competing Ulster 'selves' managed to squeeze out the socialists. Wright points to the divisive role of the 'Labour Unionists' created by the Unionist leadership by the expulsions of Catholics and 'rotten Prods' (socialists) from the shipyards, amid republican violence. In the infant Czechoslovakia, by contrast, the strength of the social democrats among Bohemian Germans played a restraining role in preventing the eruption of national conflict and ensuring the Czech majority took a liberal line - though, tragically, this accommodation was not to last.[6]

The second world war and the early post-war period were to be the high-point for Labour in Northern Ireland. It is easy to dismiss the efforts of the labour movement in the region, given sectarian labour-market inequalities and the manner in which the Northern Ireland Labour Party could be torn apart by an issue as insignificant as (in the 1960s!) whether swings should be untied on Sundays. But Terry Cradden has done a great service in rescuing the pragmatic efforts of many activists and leaders over the Stormont decades, in very difficult circumstances, to steer an accommodationist course.[7]

And this was not without its successes. It was pressure from labour in the round which brought the demise of two Unionist prime ministers: Andrews, over his Blimpish failure to prosecute the war in the early 1940s; and Brookeborough, over mass unemployment in the late 1950s and early 1960s.

Making cosmopolitanism stick

With its 'troubles' renewed in the wake of the civil rights movement, Northern Ireland was to be widely seen as a unique throwback to the seventeenth-century

---

6. Frank Wright, *Northern Ireland: A Comparative Analysis*, Dublin 1997.
7. Terry Cradden, *Trade Unionism, Socialism and Partition*, Belfast 1993.

wars of religion. Yet in many ways its divisions were a foreshadowing of the revival of ethnic conflict in Europe after the fall of the Wall.

While most on the European left saw the demise of Stalinism as the removal of an incubus from their shoulders, the collapse of this 'grand narrative' also left a vacuum. In many of the old communist states this was filled by a host of particularistic ideologies - including, in the case of former Yugoslavia, ugly and competing ethno-nationalisms, which, as in Northern Ireland, were to consume the country and many of its inhabitants. As Hobsbawm wryly put it in his summational *The Age of Extremes: The Short Twentieth Century 1914-1991*, 'the old chickens of Versailles' were 'once again coming home to roost'.

So, is enlightenment universalism - of which socialism, along with liberalism, is an offshoot - dead, as many were quickly to claim? Not quite. Happily, there are intellectual resources beyond a relativist post-modernism. Ernesto Laclau makes an important distinction between the end of the universal political actor - such as the Proletariat with its historically programmed destiny of 'dictatorship' over the rest of society - and the end of universal political *values*. Far from the latter being redundant, Laclau argues, 'the very emergence of particularistic identities means that the particular groups will have to coexist with other groups in larger communities, and this coexistence will be impossible without the assertion of values that transcend the identities of all of them'.[8]

What are these universal values that can provide the impetus for a modern socialism that is able to address ethnic division? The best answer we have is the case for 'cosmopolitanism', advanced by David Held, which builds on but transcends the historic contribution of the Austro-Marxists - still however offering a radical solution appropriate to the 'democratic framework' and 'spirit of mutual tolerance' which Heinz Fischer described.[9]

In common parlance, cosmopolitanism often conveys a sense of rootlessness, but Held gives it a precise definition, comprising three interrelated elements. First, it entails an 'egalitarian individualism', where the individual - not the state or other particular associations - is the unit of moral worth and the whole of humankind is deemed to comprise a single moral realm. Secondly, it implies

---

8. Ernesto Laclau (ed), *The Making of Political Identities*, London 1994.
9. David Held, 'From executive to cosmopolitan multilateralism', in David Held and Mathias Koenig-Archibugi (eds), *Taming Globalization: Frontiers of Governance*, Cambridge 2003.

'reciprocal recognition', in the sense that this equal moral worth is recognised by everyone. And, thirdly, it requires that each person enjoy 'impartial treatment' of their claims by public authorities, which therefore must have a 'lay' or neutral character. Together, these principles provide for peaceful coexistence in a diverse world, in just the same way as their opposites - inequality, communalism and competition for state control - are, in combination, sure-fire guarantees of ethnic conflict.

Cosmopolitanism balances private autonomy with a common public sphere where dialogue can take place in a secure context. It allows cultural diversity to be combined with at least a thin civic allegiance. As Jürgen Habermas argued, in relation to a European constitution, 'democratic citizenship establishes an abstract, legally mediated solidarity between strangers'.

Can this work? Well, it is worth looking more closely at ex-Yugoslavia here, as not everywhere did in fact erupt in ethnic flames during the 1990s. Tuzla in Bosnia-Hercegovina was a prime example of an enclave of peace amid the ravages of war. At a Council of Europe seminar in 2003, researchers from ex-Yugoslavia, and the social-democrat mayor of Tuzla Jasmim Imamovic, explained how this had been sustained. Society in the town was quite integrated by Bosnian standards, with one in four marriages ethnically mixed. The social democrats (the reformed Communists) had done well in elections in 1990 and there was a broader inter-ethnic municipal leadership committed to peace.

Mr Imamovic described their values thus: 'anti-nationalism was the highest form of patriotism'. And this took practical effect: no one was killed by the nationalistic forces during the war and even the crime rate did not rise amid all the surrounding anarchy. When a Serbian Orthodox church in the town was attacked, the council ensured that the church - 'our' church, as Mr Imamovic, from the Muslim community, tellingly described it - was repaired within three days in an important demonstration of civic leadership.

Interestingly, this approach has found its way into the new policy framework on community relations for Northern Ireland (that's the one the ethno-nationalist parties could not agree on when they had their brief shotgun marriage of devolution between 1999 and 2002), recently issued by the now direct-rule administration. This, notably, does not adopt the communalist language of 'parity of esteem' (which can only lead to what the former deputy first minister Séamus Mallon has aptly described as the 'Balkanisation' of

Northern Ireland). Rather, it defines the policy goal in cosmopolitan terms as:

> The establishment over time of a normal, civic society, in which all individuals are considered as equals, where differences are resolved through dialogue in the public sphere, and where all people are treated impartially. A society where there is equity, respect for diversity and a recognition of our interdependence.[10]

This is by no means misplaced idealism. Far from cosmopolitanism being seen as the exclusive preserve of a globalised business elite, as Chan Kwok-Bun puts it, we can 'look to the unspectacular, practical, everyday life activities that allow movement beyond group identities to the business of simply living together and solving practical problems collectively'.[11]

This is the 'good side' of that recurrent socialist call in Northern Ireland for a focus on 'bread-and-butter issues'. In reality, the old idea that these could supplant communalist claims on the political agenda was premised on an outmoded economic and class determinism. As the Austro-Marxists were the first to realise, the priority must be reversed: the constitutional argument must be seriously addressed if a left-wing socio-economic agenda is not to be ghettoised.

Developing cross-communal civic associations, particularly through the trade unions and the voluntary sector, is a key weapon in tackling ethnocentrism. The trade union tradition in Tuzla was a strong one; and in Northern Ireland the 1993 peace marches organised by the trade unions played a key role in bringing about the ceasefires a year later - something that has not been properly recognised by those blinkered by a narrow focus on the political and paramilitary elite.

Similarly, for all that Belfast is a highly segregated city, one area stands out as having survived the 'troubles' as a neighbourhood integrated in religious and social-class terms: Ballynafeigh. Why should this be? One factor is ecumenical church networks, which were apparently instigated by a radical priest in the 1960s.

---

10. Office of the First Minister and Deputy First Minister, *A Shared Future: Policy and Strategic Framework for Good Relations in Northern Ireland*, www.asharedfutureni.gov.uk.
11. In Steven Vertovec and Robin Cohen (eds), *Conceiving Cosmopolitanism: Theory, Context, and Practice*, Oxford 2004.

But another, as the *Belfast Telegraph* reported in May 2005, is the local community association, initiated at the height of polarisation in 1973 by a group of residents who wanted to form an organisation which would preserve the cultural mix of the area. As one 77-year-old resident, Martha Edmonson, put it: 'There is a great sense of community here. When the community house was established, it really helped to bring people together.'

'the *mutual commitment to ethnic protagonism ensured that power-sharing was based on the premise that 'high fences make good neighbours''*

From my own period living in the area, I know that there was strong local reaction to an attempt by the Ulster Defence Association to redefine it as 'loyalist' during the 'marching season' - by painting the kerbstones red, white and blue along the Ormeau Road overnight. This reaction was reflected, as all too rarely elsewhere, by a Department of Environment clean-up before the summer was out. The area's 'neutrality' was never again threatened.

Blood - or civic principles

Michael Ignatieff summed up the politics associated with the wars in ethnic Yugoslavia (and the Northern Ireland 'troubles') in the title of his 1994 book *Blood and Belonging: Journeys into the New Nationalism*. What Charles Leadbeater and Geoff Mulgan have called the politics of civic principles represents the progressive alternative.[12] If ethno-nationalism can be characterised as fundamentally conservative (though it does have some 'left' adherents of the Milosevic type), the politics of civic principles chimes with today's diverse, individualised society rather than one sharply divided into roughly homogeneous social blocs. It is premised on the idea that intercultural life is possible, even desirable, for individual autonomy and social dynamism. It seeks to ameliorate the associated tensions through dialogue, while developing civic engagement and social solidarity.

Above all, it sees in politics a task of civic leadership, driven by universalistic norms. It is no accident that by far the most popular political figures across the globe in the recent past - from Mary Robinson to Vaclav Havel to Nelson Mandela - have been liberal-left figures widely perceived as rising above the grubby world of

---

12. Charles Leadbeater and Geoff Mulgan, 'Lean democracy and the leadership vacuum', *Demos Quarterly* 3, 1994.

political trade-offs to embody larger ideals. Such leaders, according to Leadbeater and Mulgan, 'constantly find within history new lessons and qualities which can be applied to the future' and 'see identity as malleable and necessarily changing to cope with shifting circumstances'. By contrast, they go on: 'At the other extreme are politicians who regard history and identity as closed and fixed. As a result they believe the point of politics is to live out a society's sense of historic destiny.'

The four parties that were to form the ill-fated Executive Committee at Stormont, when devolution eventually took place, came to the negotiating table in 1997 with just such dogmatic and partisan stances. Sinn Féin (SF) was in denial about devolution at all; the SDLP preferred joint London-Dublin authority over Northern Ireland, in which the assembly would only be consultative; the Ulster Unionist Party wanted only (initial) Welsh-style administrative devolution, where proportionately allocated assembly chairs would become heads of departments; and the DUP (by now outside the talks because SF was in) hankered after some kind of majority rule.

All proffered constitutional demands which were obviously convenient for the promotion of ethnic goals (SF and the DUP) or at least for blocking those of the 'other side' (the SDLP and UUP). None, in short, favoured anything as uncertain as an assembly with primary legislative powers and a power-sharing cabinet (as had the non-confessional parties). But while none of the communal parties proposed that for which they eventually settled, their *mutual* commitment to ethnic protagonism ensured that the *form* of power-sharing adopted was based on the premise 'high fences make good neighbours', thereby containing the seeds of its own destruction.

The key elements of the architecture reproduced the so-called 'consociationalist' scheme long advocated by the Dutch political scientist Arend Lijphart.[13] This type of administration involves a grand-coalition government with inbuilt communal vetoes, while on the ground communal segregation is sustained.

The alternative to such conservative communalism is, as I have indicated, a civic cosmopolitanism which recognises the uniqueness and complexity of

---

13. These included, among others, 'communal registration', whereby assembly members were required to 'designate' themselves as 'unionist', 'nationalist' or 'other', to assist in measures to ensure 'cross-community support' for 'key decisions', as, for example, in the 'parallel consent' procedure. This required that any successful resolution be supported by a majority of the 'unionist' and 'nationalist' blocs.

each of our identities, developing as they do in relationship with one another and with an associated capacity for change. This implies an integrationist model of power-sharing, where the aim is to build coalitions of the moderate middle and to incentivise conciliatory politics, while pursuing initiatives in the wider society - such as integrated education - which over time can lead to a more 'normal' civic society emerging.

I t is not hard to see that the interests of liberals and socialists lie with the latter rather than with the former. Consociationalist power-sharing tends to reproduce communalist mindsets and entrench division, thereby delegitimising intercommunal parties and crowding out any debate on the public interest or the common good. That is why the liberal Alliance Party has struggled, having *apparently* with the Belfast agreement achieved its historic goal, and Labour is fragmented and marginal.

Corroding the blocs

An integrationist project for constitutional reform, as Rick Wilford and I have argued, would in essence be the opposite of joint authority.[14] Bottom-up rather than top-down, it would seek to corrode, rather than entrench, the 'logic of the blocs' between unionism and nationalism. It would argue for civic allegiance to a neutral 'state' in Northern Ireland, based on an egalitarian system of power-sharing which had the capacity to evolve over time towards a 'normal' left-right divide. It would comprise a cosmopolitan, 'both-and', rather than an 'either-or' approach to the wider Irish and British (and European) contexts. It should be capable of securing substantial support in Northern Ireland, as a pragmatic approach which goes with the grain of today's world, as well as wider endorsement across these islands, where nearly eight years on from the agreement the region's communalist politics provoke ever greater *ennui* - as reflected in the plummeting electoral participation which the Electoral Commission reported in 2005.

In detail this suggests four reforms:

♦ affirmation of the *sui generis* constitutional character of Northern Ireland, to move the agenda beyond the continuing (indeed intensifying) unionist-nationalist antagonism;

14. Rick Wilford and Robin Wilson, *A Route to Stability: The Review of the Belfast Agreement*, Belfast 2003, www.democraticdialogue.org/working/agreview_files/agreview.pdf.

- reconsideration of the assembly electoral system (PR-STV), to favour cross-communal vote-pooling, rather than separate intra-Protestant and intra-Catholic contests with their 'ethnic outbidding';
- removal of the requirement for assembly members to designate as 'unionist' or 'nationalist', which entrenches sectarian mindsets and delegitimises 'others';
- changing executive formation from the d'Hondt mechanism (which enforced proportionality, and hence required no effort to build trust), to inter-party agreement and subsequent collective responsibility.

To look at just the last of these in more detail, this would take us beyond the - again ethnically partisan - contemporary argument between those favouring the maintenance of d'Hondt (SF and the SDLP) as against a 'voluntary coalition' (DUP). What is needed, as in every other democratic society, *particularly* those that are ethnically divided, is an *agreed* coalition which complies with the requirements of equal citizenship and dialogue. One way of doing this would be to require that government in Northern Ireland was equally balanced, in the 'objective' sense of the monitoring of religious background for fair-employment purposes (while not excluding individuals from ethnic minorities or ignoring gender balance). This would incentivise parties to moderate their stances, to ensure that a more conciliatory intracommunal rival would not scoop the pool at the cabinet table for their 'side' - in contrast to the current pressures towards ethnic outbidding.

There would be a strong case in this context for removing the limits in the agreement on the areas in which north-south co-ordination can take place in Ireland. In a cosmopolitan perspective, it is *both* highly desirable to engage in policy networks involving the other UK jurisdictions (particularly in a devolved context) *and* for a new Stormont assembly to be able to collaborate with Dáil Eireann on any issue on which there is all-Ireland agreement (arguably even including the 'reserved' and 'excepted' areas). This would in a sense mean the coexistence of Northern Ireland in a United Kingdom and a united Ireland at one and the same time, and would undermine the rationale for the maintenance of unionist and nationalist parties. Within that context there should be a return towards the centre, with the SDLP and UUP redefining themselves as a genuinely social-democratic and labour party on the one hand

and a Northern Ireland Christian democratic party on the other.

During 2006, Democratic Dialogue hopes to take this debate forward by organising a 'Forum on the Future'. Unlike the approach by government to the politics of Northern Ireland, which is running into the sand, this would engage civil society as well as the elite, would be public rather than private, would be focused on deliberation rather than negotiation, and would start from the premise of 'a shared future' rather than the mutually exclusive wish-lists of the protagonists.

Conclusion

Such a new constitutional project could provide a vehicle to unify and strengthen the progressive political forces in Northern Ireland - the 'social-democratic' and labour wing of the SDLP, the two Labour groupings (one British-, one Irish-oriented), Alliance and the Greens - without asking them to abandon their red, yellow or green causes. If realised, it would engender a form of governance in which intercommunal parties would become pivotal to government formation by agreement, and to the policy direction of the wider society, now placed on a path towards integration. It would therefore create a platform for the further growth of progressive politics in the future.

Is Northern Ireland's liberal left capable of rising to this challenge? It has little future if it does not. And it could break out of the political ghetto in which it currently finds itself by setting the agenda for the wider society in a way it has been unable to do since the civil rights movement.

There are lessons here for the British left. For many decades, the language of anti-racism served its cause - and served it very well, given the extent and depth of discrimination and inequality it sought to counter (and still needs to counter). But this discourse finds itself more and more limited in addressing the kinds of intra- and interethnic tensions that have been seen, for example, in two recent episodes in Birmingham: the effective censorship by male Sikh elders of a play by a young Sikh woman and the Handsworth riots - this time pitting Afro-Caribbeans against Asians rather than blacks against white police.

The Austro-Marxists were ultimately unable to solve such problems with the political vocabulary they had to hand. In this regard, civic cosmopolitanism may provide a more robust alternative to conservative communalism for the twenty-first century left.

Pensions and the growth of Israel

Richard Minns

Richard Minns shows how a completely transformed approach to Histradut funds reflects the new priorities of the Israeli state.

Everything in Israel is seen through the perspective of the conflict between Arabs and Jews, regardless of whether or not that gets to the truth of the actual issues. Take pensions, as big an issue in Israel as in the EU or other regions. Outside Israel, the problem is named as an excess of old people over tax-paying workers. In Israel, the demographic issue is named as the potential excess of Arabs over Jews within Israel, especially 'greater Israel'. If Israel continues its expansion into Palestine, thus incorporating more Arabs, that threat of losing Jewish numerical and economic supremacy (see table 1 on next page) within the state of Israel becomes a reality.

But a different, and usually buried, perspective was brought into the open when Amir Peretz, the head of Israel's trade union federation Histadrut, replaced Shimon Peres as the leader of the Labour Party in Israel's governing coalition in 2005. Although Peretz had no international reputation at the time, he was known to British trade unionists. A year earlier, in September 2004, he had told a TUC fringe meeting what he had been saying in Israel: that there were two wars going on; one was with the Palestinians, the other was between Histadrut and the government, which now saw the unions as the enemy of the state. Yet, said Peretz, 'we have the biggest gap in the world in Israel between rich and poor, bigger even than the USA'. The betrayal is particularly acute, as Israel's huge pension fund, historically controlled by Histadrut, has for decades provided vital extra resources for assimilating new immigrants and easing

Table 1: Demography/Geography

(a) Age breakdown 2001, %

	0-14	15-64	65+
Israel 100	27.6	62.6	9.7
West Bank/Gaza 100	46.6	50.1	3.3

(b) Population growth rate, 1980-2001, %

Israel	2.4
West Bank/Gaza	3.5*

*figures vary; this is an average for the period.

(c) Population forecast, from 2004 to 2015, millions

	2004	2015
Israel	6.78	7.9
West Bank/Gaza	3.78	4.8

(d) Ethnic/religious breakdown on 2004 figures, millions, estimates

	2004 total	Arab	Others	Total Jew/Arab
Israel	6.78	1.3	0.6*	4.88***
West Bank/Gaza	3.78	3.78 (plus 1.3)	1.0**	6.08

* no religion, non-Arab Christians (0.3), non-Jewish Russians (0.3)
** returnee refugees (figure has a wide margin either way)
*** figures exclude 0.4 million Jewish settlers

(e) Palestine: effects of Jewish immigrants on indigenous Palestinian population

	Palestinians	%	Jews	%	
1870	367,224	98	7,000	2	Small native Jewish population
1912	525,000	93	40,000	6	Immigration started 1880s
1925	598,000	83	120,000	17	Mass increase after WWI
1946	1,237,000	65	608,000	35	Just before Partition Plan
2004	6,080,000	57	4,880,000	43	See previous table on ethnicity

Sources; various, including personal calculations

economic adjustment during rapid economic development.

Hegemony of Labour Zionism

Histadrut has been a central character in the formation of the development of Israel, so powerful it has sometimes been referred to as a state within a state. It had the controlling voice over the health and pensions services and, at one time, about one third of the economy. Labour Zionism, meaning that organised labour would be the core of the making of Israel, was the summation of all the Zionisms.

Developing close alignment with Israel's Labour government, Histadrut had become, by the 1990s, an industrial holding company, finance provider, quasi-political party, promoter of industrial and agricultural co-operatives, and pension fund manager. Yet Histadrut's role in making Israel had undergone significant shifts since its founding conference in 1920. Its first resolution affirmed its purpose as 'to build a Jewish workers' society'. Using the language of, and sharing much experience with, other workers' movements, it was a member of the Second International. But it was refused membership of the Third International because it was deemed to subordinate class struggle to nationalism - a dilemma which was to haunt it. The dilemma provoked attack from the state when the balance was seen to tip towards class rather than nationalism; and from the left (especially in other countries) when it was reported that Histadrut was involved in the manufacture of weapons, or was discriminating against Palestinian labour, or was withholding its approval of industrial action which threatened its self-interest.

Zeev Sternhell, the Leon Blum Professor of Political Science at the Hebrew University, Jerusalem, and author of *The Founding Myths of Israel; Nationalism, Socialism and the Making of the Jewish State* (Princeton 1998), argues that in Histadrut: 'socialism became merely a tool of national aims, and the labour movement unhesitatingly took the path of nationalist socialism. This explains the fact, it is argued, that the Histadrut made no large-scale attempt to create a society essentially different from a normal capitalist one' (p19).

In the 1950s Histadrut had become arguably the most powerful organisation in Israel, running the health service and the country's pension system prior to, and subsequently alongside, the state national insurance system which was established in 1954 as the National Insurance Institute. Histadrut sponsored kibbutzim, co-operative enterprises, union-owned enterprises, educational services, transport and distribution systems. One-third of the workforce became trade union members of Histadrut. Often jointly with the Jewish Agency and the Jewish National Fund, it owned companies and utilities, with part state ownership in some cases. Many of these activities were channelled through a special economic branch - Hevrat Ovdim - dedicated to creating employment and productive activities; it also had a movement for working women - Na'amat; and a youth movement - Hano'ar Ha'Oved v'Halomed. It also owned Bank Hapaolim (the Workers' Bank), with co-operative loan funds and savings funds. The bank was the largest Israeli bank after Bank Leumi, which was run directly by the World Zionist Organisation (WZO).

As well as being seen as a state within a state, Histadrut was also known, prior to 1948, as the pre-State state or the 'proto-state'.[1] It had parallel party elections to the state itself. Prior to 1995, Histadrut's leadership was part of the Labour Party leadership and leaders of Histadrut were like parallel Prime Ministers; David Ben-Gurion, the first Prime Minister of Israel, was Secretary General of Histadrut for more than ten years. At that time, the dominant *Labour* Zionism embedded a distinctly progressive stance in the new state. As Sternhell points out: 'like all nationalist movements fighting for independence, and like all nationalist parties struggling to attain office in their respective countries, the Jewish national movement understood the necessity of a progressive social policy'. Under Histadrut, a partially funded, defined benefit pension scheme evolved, which covered most non-public sector workers.[2] From 1953 to 1957, 60 per cent of Histadrut pension funds were invested in Hevrat Ovdim enterprises. After 1957 a proportion went into special

---

1. Ram Chermesh, *A State within a State: Industrial Relations in Israel, 1965-1987*, Greenwood Press 1993; Adam Hanieh, 'From State-Led Growth to Globalisation: The Evolution of Israeli Capitalism', *Journal of Palestine Studies*, Vol. XXXII (No 4, Summer 2003), p6.

2. A note on pension definitions: 'funded' means contributions from employers and/or employees are 'invested' in securities (shares, bonds or deposits) in a 'fund', with a view to the payment of pensions in the future; 'defined benefit' means that the pensions are calculated according to some explicit formula known, or defined, in advance; 'pay-as-you-go' means that benefits are paid directly out of contributions or taxation - there is no 'fund'; 'defined contribution' means pensions are dependent on the amount of the contributions and the investment returns from them. They are 'funded'.

Treasury bonds at a preferential interest rate, thereby subsidising the funds. The proportions to be invested in such bonds grew from 60 per cent to over 90 per cent by the early 1960s. All funds were transferred through Bank Hapaolim, which generated further income for Histadrut. Benefit formulae were generous in terms of years of contribution, one aim initially being to offer very generous pensions to the huge numbers of new Jewish immigrants. Immigration was a key tenet of the WZO; it was the fundamental element in the growth of the Jewish population, and the solution to the demographic question, for many decades in the twentieth century.

Banks were also instructed to finance the government deficit by purchasing government bonds. Interlocking banking and insurance (both of which included the pension funds) meant that there was virtually a state-directed core economic grouping, or state economic conglomerate, designed to develop the new state through workers' pension contributions and personal savings. In sum, the banks and the large Histadrut pension funds were financial arms of a political movement, not institutions motivated primarily by profit. In this sense critics of Histadrut, who allege it was capitalist because it pursued profit, are wrong. It was not capitalist and not profit-maximising. It was nationalist and corporatist. Of course there were capitalists, just as there were socialists, within the structure. But since the mode of production was not the issue, it could be attacked by socialists as well as capitalists for its nationalist orientation.

Pension fund as an arm of Zionism

The pension funds were crucial. They had grown in size and importance earlier and faster than pension funds in any other society that comes to mind. They began in the 1930s under the British Mandate as provident funds, with employers and employees each contributing three per cent rising to five per cent, and based on collective agreements. The funds were initially managed by a bank or by the employing company. In the 1940s Histadrut introduced general provident funds (Mivtachim for blue collar workers, Le'Pakid for administrative employees, and an insurance fund for construction workers). In the 1950s each general provident fund established a pension fund with its own administration and investment facility. For Histadrut pensions, the most significant development was the establishment of the Central Pension Fund for Histadrut Workers (Keren Hagimlaot Hamerkazit) in 1954.

The most important impetus in these developments was the national collective agreement of 1964 between Histadrut and the Manufacturers' Association, which required all employers in the association to join the Histadrut Mivtachim pension fund. Two years later the agreement was extended to all industrial enterprises, confirming Histadrut's judgement in a 2004 mimeograph that the practice of collective bargaining created Israel's pension system.

In the same document, Histadrut stressed its aim of comprehensiveness and inter-generational solidarity:

> It should be emphasised that one of the primary characteristics of the pension funds, and the main difference between them and other providers of insurance, is the obligation of the pension funds to accept as members *all workers* employed in a plant that has joined the fund voluntarily, or been compelled to join, as well as a worker who has begun to work in the plant after it has joined the fund. In effect, a pension fund is not able to choose its members. In this way, the social pension funds have an intergenerational obligation - the new generation of workers joining the fund finance and enable the veteran members to enjoy pension rights. Without this continuity, the foundation allowing for the very existence of the pension fund is damaged. This important principle has constituted a central layer in the Histadrut policy as the workers' representative and as an organisation that wishes to guarantee pension security for everyone.

This is amazing stuff for the European pension systems which have been going through the new ideology of privatisation and personal pension accounts for the last ten years. Histadrut has mastered all the arguments. The reasons for doing so are interesting. A telling aspect of Histadrut's pension fund philosophy was that:

> The pension funds never served solely as a 'savings fund' ... the pension funds served as an instrument for applying the national and social policies of state institutions. Throughout the years - and in accordance with dictated government policy - the funds acted to benefit various populaces, such as new immigrants. In fact the benefits provided to various populaces were in

line with the approach of the pension scheme (which was different ... from other contractual commercial arrangements).

Indeed, Histadrut played an instrumental role in immigration policy for decades. This occurred despite restrictions on immigration imposed by the British under the Mandate from 1922 onwards. Altogether about 125,000 'illegal' immigrants arrived in Palestine between 1934 and 1948, bringing the population of the new state of Israel in 1949 to 716,000 Jews and 92,000 Arabs, with 700,000 Arabs having fled as refugees. Two key agencies in the immigration activity were the Hagana (forerunner of the IDF - Israeli army), and a 'centre for illegal immigrants' (Mosad le-Aliya Bet) founded specifically for the purpose. These organisations were closely associated with Histadrut. The activity of the Histadrut pension fund fits logically into this national objective.

Deficits and demographic politics

During the 1980s, it was claimed that the Histadrut pension funds had accumulated large actuarial deficits of over 100 billion NIS (New Israel Shekels; 1$US = 4.7 NIS). The reasons were said to be fourfold, as summarised by Histadrut:

♦ Increasing longevity: life expectancy for the male population was 70.3 years in 1975; in 1985 it reached 73.5; and in 2000, 76.7; life expectancy of women was 73.4 years in 1975; 77.4 in 1985; and 80.9 in 2000. It was concluded that, taking the post-retirement years for which pensions are payable, the timescale had doubled, with no corresponding increase in assets.

♦ The role of women: the growth in women's labour force participation rates and pension fund membership had a further impact, compounded by women being able to retire at 60, and having greater longevity.

♦ Changes in the determining salary: during the 1980s many different wage components contributed to the calculation of pension benefits, while the contributions were made on a different basis.

♦ Government policy: the government required the pension funds to provide improved pension terms to various groups, for example: to encourage immigration, the government wanted new immigrants to be entitled to a reasonable old-age pension, rather than placing the burden on the National

Insurance Institute. Since many new immigrants began to accumulate pension rights at a relatively advanced age, they were given the option of an accelerated accumulation of pension rights (doubling the yearly rate of accumulation to 4 per cent during the first 10 years). This was only reversed in 1989. The unemployed were also granted an accelerated accumulation of pension rights, despite extended periods during which they were unable to pay contributions.

In line with this use of the Histadrut pension fund to further national economic development, the government also provided special benefits for its own workers - either by reducing insurance premiums or by other means - and passing on provision for groups of civil servants to the Histadrut funds.

Table 2; Old Age Crisis; longevity and dependency; Israel and various international comparisons (%)

	Israel	Comparator
(i) Expected duration of retirement at official retirement age	*(1988)*	*(Countries (15) with per cap GDP greater than $8000 (various years in 1980s))*
Men	15.1	15.2
Women	20.7	18.6
(ii)	*(1990)*	*(OECD (1990))***
Population over 60	12.1	18.6 (18.2*)
Population over 65	8.9	13.6 (13.2*)
(iii)		
Population over 65/population 15-64	14.9	20.4 (19.6*)
Population over 60/population 20-59	25.6	34.0 (32.9*)

** excl. Turkey
*weighted average

Source; *Averting the Old Age Crisis; Policies to Protect the Old and Promote Growth* (World Bank, 1994), Tables A10 for (i), A1 for (ii) and (iii).

Table 2 shows the longevity and old-age dependency comparisons for Israel, and the averages for comparable countries. The longevity issue for women is certainly apparent. However, the old age dependency issue, so prevalent as the cause of concern in most other countries, but not mentioned in the Histadrut case, is not; and this could be seen, in social accounting terms, as a positive counterbalance to the general 'actuarial deficit'.

Actuarial science is inexact to say the least. Like many other 'scientific' assessments of social affairs, the structure of the investigation (and hence, for example, the way deficit is defined), can depend on what you want to prove or disprove. There is a substantial ongoing debate about actuarial methodology. 'Deficit' is a term which has varied in importance and relevance over time. Sometimes the concept of 'bankruptcy' is bandied about as well - a term from company law and accountancy that is not necessarily relevant when analysing a pension scheme, where, for example, social accounting is part of the picture. Terms such as deficit and bankruptcy are part of the language of financial sciences, and are products of the social structures they are designed to measure; they are not some kind of deus ex machina.

Broadly speaking, successive governments over more than thirty years used Histadrut funds as an additional means of assimilating new immigrants, and easing economic adjustment during rapid economic development for both the public and private sectors. Depending on the 'scientific' approach adopted for assessing these expenditures - in other words depending on political priorities - they could simply be regarded as 'exceptional items', and accounted for differently. But when it came to a general attack on Histadrut, they were not.

Embrace of neo-liberalism

The reassessment of pension fund policies occurred during the 1980s, firstly during a Likud-Labour coalition, and later under Yitzhak Rabin's Labour government, culminating in 1995 when Labour lost control of Histadrut's governing body for the first time in its history. The appearance of the actuarial deficits in the pension funds had coincided with a wholesale shift in politics and economics. Immigration as a source of Jewish population growth had shrunk due to economic, social and political difficulties in Israel and the continuous wars. Net migration (immigration minus emigration) as a percentage of population growth was 68.9 per cent in the years 1948 to 1960; 45 per cent to 1971; 25 per cent to 1982; and just 6.3 per cent to 1986. The policies shifted to the encouragement of natural growth, in terms of population increase ('the war of the cradles' explored by Youssef Courbage[3]), and in terms of territory. The expanding occupation of the West Bank and the extension of settler communities became a financial and political priority. This was set against a background of the financial crisis of the early 1980s, which led to three-digit inflation and culminated in the nationalisation of the banks. All of this accompanied a momentous loss of Labour's decades-old hegemony. After Labour lost the national election for the first time in 1977, all of the old Labour-controlled structures were up for examination.

T he pension fund had served its purpose. For the first time in forty years, 'conventional', but subjective actuarial concepts were applied to the Histadrut pension funds and revealed a crisis. Proposals were made by a special commission to close the funds to new members, establish new funds and introduce new benefit formulae. It was also proposed to change the requirement to invest over 90 per cent of the funds in special non-tradable government bonds. This requirement was reduced to 30 per cent, with the balance of 70 per cent to be invested in the Tel Aviv and other stock markets and alternative investments. No more special bonds with their subsidy for Histadrut pension funds were to be issued.

The transformation of the Histadrut funds met with strong opposition and threats of strikes. The confrontations culminated in a general strike in 1997, even under the new, non-Labour Histadrut, following government reneging on certain pension undertakings. In 2003 a new government bill provided a settlement for all the pension funds, annulling all previous accords and decisions, in the context of a 'Recovery Plan for the Israeli Economy'. The Histadrut pension funds were nationalised, with the Treasury taking over interim control prior to them being

---

3. Youssef Courbage, 'Reshuffling the Demographic Cards in Israel/Palestine', *Journal of Palestine Studies*, Vol XXIII, No 4 (Summer 1999). The article also presents interesting insights into the demographic implications of the ethnic split within the Jewish population itself.

sold off. The old funds were closed and new funds were established for new members, and shifted on to a defined contribution basis. The new investment rules applied to old and new funds alike, and to all other pension funds.

Other non-Histadrut pension funds were not nationalised. These other pension funds were comparatively small. They took the form of provident funds run by banks, the legacy of the original pension idea from the 1930s, similar to personal pension plans, mutual funds or unit trusts that we know about in the UK. But the Histadrut pension funds were the main target and instrument of government policy; they controlled 80 per cent of the institutional market (Mivtachim over 50 per cent, Makefet, 17 per cent, others 10 per cent). I estimate the size of the market at $30 billion, equivalent to a third of GDP. The market was heavily concentrated in terms of control, as it is elsewhere, but in Israel there were the conglomerates of banks and insurance companies with their cross-holdings and oligopolistic control, in which five conglomerates dominated the economy. Histadrut was the hub of the structure.

The government's plan was to break up this concentration of control along with the dominance of Histadrut. The new functions to be performed for the economy and the state were the expansion of the stock market (which first emerged in 1985), the provision of greater access to 'independent' portfolio managers, and wholesale privatisation of utilities and state economic interests. Israel wanted to emerge from what it thought was a developing economy status into a developed one, by implementing what can only be characterised as the neo-liberal agenda. 'Economic rationality' was to replace 'ideological beliefs', as Yair Aharoni put it.[4] The issue was not a Histadrut-pensions crisis, but a fundamental shift in politics and economics.

Stock market politics and economics

By the year 2000 Israel had won a classification from the FTSE (Financial Times Stock Exchange index) as an Advanced Emerging Market, along with Greece, Brazil, South Korea, Mexico, South Africa and Taiwan. Israel (Tel Aviv Stock Exchange - TASE) was also included in the FTSE All-World Index.

The absence of a 'free capital market' had made Israel's economy stand

---

4. 'The Changing Political Economy of Israel', *Annals of the American Academy of Political and Social Science*, 555, Jan 1998.

out in the listings of capitalist economies. To begin with, TASE and the Israeli financial markets generally were completely dominated by the state as the chief mobiliser of savings and the main allocator of credit, some of which we have seen. This was the legacy of another part of Labour Zionism, and drew on a combination of a socialist-revolutionary inheritance particularly from Russian Jews, and a belief that the state was the more efficient decision-maker concerning capital investment. By 2003, no less than 56 per cent of share ownership on the TASE was still classified as 'interested parties', or cross-holdings and major group holdings, as referred to earlier. On the TASE market in 2002, pension funds had zero holdings - as would be expected from their investment history in Israel. The increase in pension fund portfolio investment was designed to change this, so that new economic groups and the continuing large privatisation programmes could raise capital. The Mivtachim funds (old and new) (the main Histadrut funds) began investing in the diversified range of holdings out of cash flow at a rate of 15-20 per cent per annum. This began to create a 10 per cent dilution of government bond holdings per year. At the same time the management of the funds was put out for private tender.

The intended new role for Histadrut and other pension funds was that they should make a positive contribution to the economy by providing investment capital instead of being classified as a bankrupt burden. But the reality is precisely the opposite. Israel's pension fund structure was significant for national assimilation and development during the 'nationalist socialist' stage, while stock market-based systems are an unproven quantity for the 'neo-liberal' stage. Pension funds elsewhere may have contributed to the expansion of financial markets through their liberalised investment powers; and they may have contributed to privatisation. But this is not the same as economic development. It is merely a means of shifting corporate ownership and control between different corporate and financial groups. This suggests that the pension reforms had more to do with a restructuring of labour power by new political constituencies, and a restructuring of the stock market away from domination by state and labour groups, than with improving pensions.

Conclusions

Our inability to extricate pensions from broader economic and political issues demonstrates how such a major area of social policy is not what it seems.

Pensions are used for purposes other than pensions. The parameters of debate are set by other political priorities and economic interests. The situation of Israel/Palestine, and the major long-term territorial and religious/ethnic conflict, provides a startling illustration of this. Pensions helped significantly in the creation of the state of Israel. It is difficult to see, on the basis of the evidence from elsewhere, how they will contribute further.

I would like to thank Andy Batkin and Bryn Davies (UK) for their detailed comments on earlier drafts, plus staff of Histadrut (Tel Aviv) for their co-operation in the research, as well as the University of Haifa, the National Insurance Institute (Jerusalem), the Knesset (Jerusalem), the Palestinian Economic Research Institute (Ramallah), the Institute of Palestine Studies (Beirut), and the Tel Aviv Stock Exchange. My assumption of personal responsibility for the end result applies as usual.

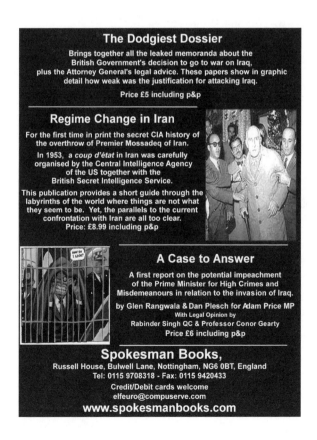

Four Poems

Playing with words at Abu Ghraib

1
Call it hazing
        that makes it a prank
Call it letting off steam
        it's understandable
Call it softening them up
        that makes it a duty
Call it stressing them out
        that's psychology
Call it interrogation
        that's expertise
Call it a few bad apples
        the rot stops there.

Call it torture
        it's only abuse
Call it violation
        stuff happens
Call it contravention
        it's 'legally available'
Call it corrupt
        it's military necessity
Call it a war crime
        they're non-legal combatants
Call it wrong
        trust us, trust us.

2
Shoes, bodies, piled up without shame
but even at Auschwitz-Birkenau the guards
taking photographs for souvenirs
didn't put themselves in the frame.

Here we have Sabrina from Tallahassee
majorette smile, perfect teeth
thumbs up beside the bashed up
shrink-wrapped Manadel al-Jamadi.

Here we have Charles and Ed
with Lynndie grinning, posing
feet planted like one of the boys
with her prisoner on a lead.

This is pay-back time, carnival
when anything's allowed and, hey,
there are words for it.
Who says? The General.

3

This is Lynndie
This is Chip
Lynndie likes fun
Chip likes fun

This is Ali
Is Ali a dog?
No Ali is not a dog
Ali is a man.

Lynndie plays with Ali
Chip plays with Ali
This is fun says Lynndie
This is fun says Chip
I like fun says Lynndie
I like fun says Chip
Ali does not like fun

Lynndie and Chip are having fun
Jump Ali jump says Lynndie
Sing Ali sing says Chip
This is fun says Lynndie
This is fun says Chip

Fuck Ali says Lynndie
Take a picture says Chip
We like fun say Lynndie and Chip
Smile says Lynndie
Fun fun fun fun fun says Chip.

Carole Satyamurti

Rats, August 2005

1
From beneath the bank
of the brook, in the first
searing days
of the drought, water

rats appeared,
two of them,
we'd never known
even were there.

Unlike city
rats skulking
in cellars or sliding
up from a sewer-

mouth - I saw this,
it wasn't dusk -
these, as blithe
as toy tanks,

sallied into the garden
to snitch the crusts
we'd set
out for the birds.

But still, who
knows what filth
and fetor and rot
down in their dark

world they were
before? I shouted
and sent them
hurtling back.

2
Now the brute
crucible of heat
has been upon us
for weeks,

just breathing is work,
and we're frightened.
The planet all
but afire, glaciers

dissolving, deserts
on the march,
hurricanes without end,
and the president

and his energy-company
cronies still insist
climate change
isn't real. The rats

rove where they will
now, shining and fat,
they've appropriated
the whole lawn.

From this close,
they look just
like their cousins
anywhere else,

devious, ruthless,
rapacious, and every
day I loathe
them more.

C. K. Williams

Prose poem

I look at you in helpless silence, incapable of doing
a thing for you. In the middle of the white-washed walls
of the hospital ward you lie, groaning quietly in the dark abyss
of pain.
Only a miracle can bring you some relief. I have nothing to offer,
but a prayer. All my prayers reach the Almighty, an attempt I
shall make.
I am trying to find ways to shake off His unbearable silence.
Desolation and numbness in your eyes drive me crazy and as
I leave the ward quietly, I hear the footsteps of death. I want
to
cut off my ears to block their sound. But will that delay the
advent of death?
From your voicelessness before death, I move towards your
silence
after death - and I do not even want to feel angry or shed tears
at my helplessness.

Suresh Dalal

Irish Mary

A binman found her, wedged in the gap between one factory
and another. She'd been shoved in there so forcefully she
sealed the narrow way and all the dead leaves and muck
skirling in the Autumn winds had gathered up against her,
shielding her from view. The man, glimpsing her black PVC
mac, had thought she was a rubbish bag. He'd reached to
tug it free and then he'd smelt her; gagging, he'd run and
got his gaffer to ring the coppers.

She'd been there a while, not too long, but long enough
for the rats and dogs to have been at what bits of her they
could get. But her face, pressed hard under the twisted arm,
was intact and the softening bloat of decay had smoothed
her wasted features so at first glance, she looked strangely
young again. It was a face she hadn't worn for years, but had
her mother, long gone, seen it, she would have wept for the
wreck of her child, the bonny little thing red as the sun,
who'd laughed and begged for sweetie money in the sour
hallways of the places they'd lived.

The copper who had the case watched as they took her
away, and wondered who she was. When he told the local
newspaper, he described her as a 'young woman' and hoped
for a headline on the front page because that might bring
her people out, might get someone to claim her. Also, the
more he knew about her, the better chance he had of
finding who had killed her, because it was murder, no doubt
of that. He knew if he said 'prostitute' it would only get a
few lines on the inside pages; whores interested no-one,
their lives were as invisible as their deaths.

Eventually, her fingerprints told her story - not a novel
one, and certainly nothing new to the copper who sat at his
battered desk and rubbed his temples trying to ease his
headache. There was no-one to claim Mary Cafferty, Dublin
Irish, convictions for soliciting, drug addict; a drifter fetched

up in this city of drifters, another voice whispering in the polyglot babble of the tumbling stone maze of Town. Irish Mary was her working name; a nickname as old as the Life. Irish Mary, Scotch Mary, Red Mary, Black Mary, Long Mary, Little Mary - all the Marys and none of them blessed, none of them redeemed, some of them mothers and none of their sons their saviours. The copper sighed and leaning back in the creaking chair, shut his eyes and meditated on the man who'd killed this Irish Mary.

Whatever the copper dreamed was near enough the truth, but not near enough to catch the man who after Mary in her shiny mac had caught his eye, had driven with her shivering in the passenger seat to the small industrial estate where at night, the girls did the business. He was not a thinking man; he wanted what he wanted when he wanted it and afterwards, it had no meaning for him. Mary had barely finished wiping her mouth before the thud of her thick Dublin brogue rang in his ears like a dull gong, begging for her money, *I want me money, where's me money, c'mon mister, where's me* ... Fucking whores, never gave a fella a second's peace. So he took hold of her neck, thin and greenish as a primrose stalk and putting his brutal thumbs up under her ears, snapped it. That shut her up, right enough.

Then, as she lolled against the door, he took her purse - may as well after all, no point throwing money away - and her cheap little thread of a gold chain with the wispy cross and Miraculous Medal, the Holy Mother stamped on it a little out of kilter, the prayer for protection unreadable. His daughter had a birthday coming up, it would do a treat and another saving made.

Then he got out, went round the car and opened the door, letting Irish Mary fall onto the black ground. Looking round, he saw the gap between the buildings and nodding in satisfaction rammed her up there hard. Grunting, he left, and forgot her by the time he'd downed his third pint at the club.

In time, Mary was cremated at the state's expense. No-one from social services checked to see if she'd been a Catholic so she was done C of E. No-one went, except the copper who sometimes attended these funerals if he could, to stand as the nearest thing to family the lost dead had.

He drove back with an old Springsteen song playing on his stereo, along the road that Irish Mary had worked. He saw, even on this raw dark afternoon, the shadows thickened with more girls; he saw more pimps cruising in better cars than his, thinking themselves little kings, their glove compartments stashed with the stuff Irish Mary had begged for as she'd begged her mammy for sherbet lemons and liquorice allsorts in the faded past.

The copper drove by the place where Mary had been found, discarded, along with the broken spikes and used condoms and knew, in his blood and bone and sinew, the exact meaning of desolation.

Joolz Denby

When was Blairism?

Tony Bennett

Deborah Lynn Steinberg and Richard Johnson (eds), *Blairism and the War of Persuasion: Labour's Passive Revolution*, Lawrence and Wishart, 2004

When - and what - was Blairism? Both questions are clearly on the agenda as the different factions within New Labour jockey for positions regarding its post-Blair future. And both merit a clear answer if that future is to restore the opportunities for a progressive politics that Blairism has so wastefully squandered. *Blairism and the War of Persuasion* is all the more welcome, then, for its timeliness. As the most comprehensive attempt that we yet have to identify the distinctive properties of Blairism and New Labour, and to place these in a longer perspective so that their effects might be measured and assessed in a historical light, it arrives on the political scene at just the right time.

Yet there is also a sense in which questions concerning the 'when' and the 'what' of Blairism are tantalisingly deferred in this study. This is because one of the larger issues on which answers depend is not fully addressed: that is, disentangling the relations between New Labour and Blairism. I am not, in saying this, telling the editors anything they don't already know. In their introduction, Deborah Steinberg and Richard Johnson underline both the importance and the difficulty of deciphering the relationships between Blairism and New Labour. In doing so they also acknowledge that their temporalities are not coincident, interpreting Blairism as a later accretion developed in the course of New Labour's first term of office.

Given this, the broader question isn't whether *Blairism and the War of*

Persuasion successfully disentangles the relations between Blairism and New Labour but whether the terms of analysis it proposes are capable of doing so in ways that might helpfully illuminate the likely dynamics of the latter when Blair leaves. The crux of the matter here concerns the framework provided by Antonio Gramsci's theory of hegemony and, more specifically, his concept of passive revolution. For while this does not inform the approach of all of the essays in the book, it does run through many of them and, more importantly, organises the editorial context in which they are brought together.

In his *Prison Notebooks*, Gramsci interprets the Italian Risorgimento as a template for his analysis of Italian fascism as a 'passive revolution'.[1] This is a revolution in name only which, in substituting direction from above for the exercise of leadership through the mobilisation of popular forces, operates as a 'revolution without revolution'. Drawing on this as a model for their own analysis, Steinberg and Johnson, in interpreting Blairism as a 'war of persuasion', intend something deeper than the accusation that Blair and No 10 seem to govern through the flim-flam of spin. The implication is rather that this aspect of Blairism's political style is a consequence of its abandonment of the longer-term need for a 'war of position' requiring real political leadership exercised throughout civil society to build support for political projects with a genuinely transformative potential. Blairism's war of persuasion is the means by which, in lieu of this, three successive Labour governments have sought to retain an adequate level of passive support for *dirigiste* programmes which, far from nourishing and building on a groundswell of active popular support, have sought instead to dismantle and disorganise grassroots politics.

This, Steinberg and Johnson suggest, has been a necessary aspect of a political programme whose principal aims have been, first, to complete the Thatcherite labour-market revolution by extending the forms of discipline it mobilised against the unionised working classes to the professional middle classes; second, to transform the socially authoritarian gender/sexual moral order of the Thatcher and Major years into a more flexible and pliable one, but one still clearly subordinated to the exigencies of a neo-liberal economic order and the refashioned subjectivities this entails; and third, to transform Tory little-Englanderism into a new form of cosmopolitan multiculturalism. These aspects

---

1. Antonio Gramsci, *Selections from the Prison Notebooks*, edited and translated by Quintin Hoare and Geoffrey Nowell-Smith, Lawrence and Wishart, 1971.

of Blairism have been underpinned by the promotion of a new conception of citizenship which seeks to replace the citizen as a member of a public by the consumer citizen whose agency is limited to the exercise of market choices. This new civic contract is also one in which the balance between civic rights on the one hand, and the duties and responsibilities of citizenship on the other, is to be transformed decisively in favour of the latter.

These themes, painted in broad outline in the introductory editorials, are then developed in convincing, and depressing, detail in the essays that follow. Highlights for me included John Clarke and Janet Newman's discussion of the changing practices of governance under New Labour and the light this throws on the rhetorical filibustering that informs its concerns with social inclusion and community cohesion, and Richard Johnson and Valerie Walkerdine's account of the implications of the new gender order for the subjectivities of young women, owing to the inordinate pressure to compete that now bears upon them. I also greatly enjoyed Michael McKinnie's discussion of New Labour arts policies - partly because of the imaginative but telling long-bow he draws in recalling Adam Smith's account of the relations between aesthetics and economy in *The Theory of Moral Sentiments*, as a means of identifying the poverty of the thinking that informs New Labour's arts policies.[2]

Liza Schuster and John Solomos's discussion of New Labour on race relations and immigration and Jeffrey Weeks's account of its record on liberalising the laws relating to sex and sexualities provide an important contrast with one another. Weeks is, on the whole, positive about New Labour's record on sexual and relationship issues, appraising this as more radical than that of any previous Labour government and, in those areas in which it has been hesitant and ambiguous, viewing this as a legitimate reflection of broader uncertainties in the culture at large. For Schuster and Solomos, by contrast, New Labour's rhetoric of a cosmopolitan multiculturalism - quite easily profiled in 'soft' policy areas like the arts - has, notwithstanding the liberalisation of some aspects of migration, served mainly as a sharp counterpoint to actual policies which, in relation to both resident minority ethic populations and migrants, especially undocumented ones, have been mainly preoccupied by considerations of exclusion and control. And, we can now add, in the wake of

---

2. Adam Smith, *Theory of Moral Sentiments* Cambridge University Press, 2003.

the quick introduction of the changed 'rules of the game' that followed the 7 July 2005 bombings, by consideration of security, too, in a form that reveals all too clearly a relish for authoritarianism on the part of the front benches.

It's worth adding that Weeks is the only contributor to take into account the balance of pubic opinion in assessing how far a democratically elected government can realistically, and legitimately, push progressive agendas that are contentious. Yet, when not bullying or insulting it - as in the notorious fictions about WMD that provided the fig-leaf of legitimacy for the illegal invasion of Iraq - New Labour's record has, on the whole, lagged behind public opinion. This is especially true of its record in relation to equality issues. While the introduction of the minimum wage should be applauded along with other measures addressing the effects of poverty in ways that Conservative governments would not have contemplated, New Labour's record in failing to tackle the increasing inequalities that are the necessary effect of the unregulated operation of labour and other markets is abysmal. It is, then, surprising that these matters receive relatively little attention from any of the contributors. An equally surprising absence is any sustained engagement with New Labour's record in managing the economy. This is strange in view of the centrality of this to New Labour's electoral successes compared to social-democratic parties in many parts of Europe, and strange too in terms of Gordon Brown's key role in managing the economy and its significance for the relationships between the Brownite and Blairite factions within New Labour and how these might unfold when Blair resigns.

When all of these caveats are acknowledged, however, the achievements of *Blairism and the War of Persuasion* are considerable. It offers a framework for debating and assessing a new political formation that matches Stuart Hall's work on Thatcherism as a form of authoritarian populism and, before that, Hall and his co-writers' commanding engagement, in *Policing the Crisis*, with the political crises of the mid-1970s.[3] But the strengths of this tradition are also the source of some unresolved difficulties. Clarke and Newman allude to these when, in their discussion of New Labour's attempt to dissolve the problem of inequality into a series of isolated and disconnected pockets of social exclusion, they state that the really

3. Stuart Hall, Chas Critcher, Tony Jefferson, John Clarke and Brian Roberts, *Policing the Crisis: Mugging, the State, and Law and Order* Macmillan, 1978.

difficult questions concern the extent to which 'the various co-opted, repressed, excluded social possibilities can become active and effective political forces' (p63). Estella Tincknell's account of the new rules, structures and internal culture now governing the Labour Party after successive reforms - and the consequences of these in both reducing party membership and discouraging active participation on the part of the remaining membership - sounds a note of similar caution regarding the ability of the Labour Party to recruit, coordinate or prove responsive to a large membership.

I t's in relation to issues of this kind that my doubts arise regarding how far the notion of 'passive revolution' can help us see what new lines of political possibility might open up when Blairism does, indeed, become history. For this notion was, in Gramsci's work, clearly aligned with the central role that was accorded to classes, and class-based political parties, as the nucleating forces in the struggle for hegemony in ways which simply no longer have the same political salience. Nor do the editors suggest otherwise. It is clear, though, that their perspective implies, as the opposite of passive revolution, a political future that is characterised by a more active revolution arising out of the dynamics of social and civic life - but without a glimmering of any sense of the form this might take or how it might be organised. This is perhaps because this way of posing the matter itself reflects a blocked political imaginary that is unable to deliver the new forms of political inventiveness that are needed for times such as these.

Love and politics

Jon Baldwin

Tim Root, *Love, Empowerment and Social Justice: Personal Relationships and Citizen Action*, Open Gate Press, 2005

Any attempt to analyse and counter today's absence of politics is to be welcomed, and Tim Root's book contributes to a psychology of political activity by suggesting that a positive view of human nature, gained through love, can play a significant role in stimulating leftist political attitudes and activity. Alternatively, a lack of love and a dearth of emotional well-being, Root argues, may be a prime contributing factor to political deficiency and apathy. His position in *Love, Empowerment and Social Justice* is that love, as manifest in parental care, close friendships, and successful relationships, can empower and motivate citizen action and political activism. Confidence in human co-operation gained through the experience of emotionally secure interactions can lead to the challenge of damaging aspects of our divided society and a move towards fairness and social justice. Root, an activist and Senior Practitioner in Social Services, supplies social, psychological, and anecdotal evidence to support his (somewhat controversial) view that 'activists are more likely to have had warm relationships with their parents, which have given them a sufficiently positive view of others to be able to sustain good adult relationships, and care for others outside their family' (p216).

This book, then, relates socio-economic problems to psychological well-being. Root extensively discusses the causes of, and potential responses to, issues such as disaffected youth, community decline, rising debt ('mortgage', he points out, literally means 'death-grip'), inequality, boredom ('one-fifth of Americans say that they are regularly "bored out of their minds"'), pollution, divorce, anger, racism, and so on. However, the treatment of some of these issues is rather uneven. For instance the appeal of chapter two, 'Urgent - Repair our Planet!', results in just nine pages, whereas the next chapter, 'Confident Parents, Secure Children' - clearly the strongest section of the book - is over seventy pages.

Root's generally sound central argument for community over individuality is affirmed by popular psychologist Oliver James in the preface: 'If only those who rule us were more likely to have read this book than, say, *The Selfish Gene*. Instead of encouraging us to live unfulfilling, empty and destructive lives, it might mean that they start trying to build a society which nurtures a far saner, better balanced existence' (pix). Any book that promotes good relationships and explains how these might be politically achieved, as well as politically beneficial, should, as James suggests, be required reading for those involved in all aspects of social policy.

Love, which can inform the recognition of social connectedness and can thereby encourage the establishment of co-operative groups by communities, is largely Root's therapy to the problems of today and of social injustice. Whilst there is undoubtedly much mileage in this solution, the old adage that 'when you have a hammer every problem looks like a nail' also rings true. Stress, inequality, crime, economic recession, poor health care, corporate corruption, environmental damage - all are to be remedied, for Root, through love and communitarian values.

Herein lies one potential difficulty with this otherwise sensible book, for Root somewhat over-idealises love and the sense of community. There is no discussion of the potential difficulties of tight familial bonds, or communal suffocation, or erosion of difference. As Zygmunt Bauman has suggested, one of the prices to pay for the privilege and security of being in a community is loss of autonomy and freedom.[1] Bauman has also argued that community means sameness and therefore the absence (or worse, elimination) of the other, of the stranger. This is apparent in Root's discussion of the contemporary other: the immigrant. He claims that politicians need to respond to 'concerns about immigration by explaining why a certain amount is helpful to fill labour shortages ... [politicians] can also respond to fears that immigrants drain public finances by explaining that they nearly all work, few are elderly, and therefore they contribute much more in tax than they receive in benefits' (p228). This reduction of an immigrant to their utility and commercial potential is not

---

1. Zygmunt Bauman, *Community: Seeking Safety in an Insecure World*, Polity 2001 p4.

entirely helpful, and, furthermore, reveals the worrying encroachment of capitalist and commodity values into Root's thinking: things, even humans, shall function (have a use-value) and things, even humans, shall have a price (an exchange-value). Root also, to my mind problematically, valorises regional and community identity over class identity and consciousness. Councils, he argues, should 'employ only local people' and the right to rent an affordable council house 'would apply only to those who had lived in the council area since childhood or settling in Britain' (p246).

In perhaps the most upsetting part of the book, Root writes that

> activists will only improve our society if they pursue achievable aims. Despite its faults, the capitalist system has shown its resilience for over two centuries. It recovers from recessions, which governments have learnt how to mitigate. It has provided increases in wealth which would have been unimaginable to earlier generations. Only a tiny minority would favour radical change to it (pxxvi).

These are difficult sentiments to agree with. On the one hand Root over-idealises community. On the other, he is not idealistic enough; certainly not in encouraging the radical change to capitalism that many activists, in Ernst Bloch's sense, *hope* for.[2]

---

2. 'Where the capitalist sum no longer works out anywhere, the bankrupt may in fact be forced to pour and spread a blot over the ledger of the whole of existence, so that the world in general looks coal-black ... All this is an even worse deception than that of the radiant facades which can no longer be kept up. The work against this, with which history continues, indeed has been continuing for a long time, leads to the matter which could be good, not as abyss, but as mountain into the future. Mankind and the world carry enough good future; no plan is itself good without this fundamental belief within it.' Ernst Bloch, *The Principle of Hope*, MIT Press 1986, p446-7.

The 1970s and after

The political economy of inflation and the crisis of social democracy

Pat Devine

Pat Devine *argues that we urgently need to find an alternative hegemonic strategy, capable of reversing the neoliberal triumph that was inaugurated in the 1970s.*

The 1970s was the decade in which the left lost its historical role as the standard bearer of freedom and progress, the role it had proudly possessed since the French Revolution. It was the decade in which the dynamic for necessary change was hegemonised by the new right. This is why the 1970s are so crucial for an understanding of the present situation and the discussion of how to transcend the dominant neoliberal ideology that is in danger of becoming the common sense of the New Millennium. Yet there exists widespread historical amnesia in relation to the political economy of the second half of the last century.

This article is an exercise in historical retrieval. It sets out the conditions that made the post-1945 Keynesian social democratic welfare state possible; analyses the crisis of social democracy that developed around the great inflation of the 1970s and the attempts to contain it; characterises the historic achievement of the Thatcherite new right as the destruction of the historic bloc of social forces on which the post-1945 consensus depended; and identifies the historic mission of New Labour as completion of the process of consolidating neoliberal ideology as the new common sense of the age, a legacy that may be inherited by the Cameron Conservatives. The article ends by suggesting that an awareness of this history is necessary if the left is to form a new historic bloc articulated around a radical democratic agenda for civil society, the state and the economy, based on ecological sustainability and social justice.

The post-war settlement, the long boom, the inevitable crisis

The mass unemployment and fascism of the inter-war period, culminating in the second world war, gave rise to the post-war settlement and the creation of the Keynesian social democratic welfare state, which cemented a new historic bloc reflecting the changed balance of social forces in the world. Much of the right had supported fascism and was discredited. The Soviet Union had borne the brunt of the war on the allied side and emerged from it economically weakened but militarily, politically and morally strengthened. It was soon to be joined by Eastern Europe and China to constitute a global alternative to capitalism. Communist and Social Democratic parties in Western Europe also emerged from the war greatly strengthened, in Continental Europe as a result of their participation in the resistance, in Britain as the Labour Party was the beneficiary of the impetus behind the implicit social contract that had underpinned the war effort.

W elfare state Keynesianism took the form of a post-war consensus around the maintenance of full employment, the creation of the major pillars of the welfare state (health, education, social services, social security and pensions), and the nationalisation of the essential industries constituting the infrastructure for an efficient capitalism (public utilities, energy, transport and communications). The only contentious issue dividing the major political parties in Britain was the nationalisation of the iron and steel industry in 1951, which was subsequently denationalised by the Conservatives in 1953 and then renationalised by Labour in 1967. Apart from this, although there were differences on less central issues, on all the major issues there was broad cross-party agreement.

Internationally, the 1944 Bretton Woods Conference had agreed on a new international order, to be operated by an International Monetary Fund and World Bank. This consisted of a fixed exchange rate regime, together with a mechanism for adjusting balance of payments disequilibria when they arose. However, Keynes's proposal that the burden of adjustment should fall equally on surplus and deficit countries was rejected by the United States. What emerged instead was an asymmetric system in which the burden fell entirely on the deficit countries, which reflected the economic dominance and interests of the United States at the time. Like domestic welfare state Keynesianism, the Bretton Woods system thus contained the seeds of its own collapse.

The post-war consensus emerging from the second world war continued in the 1950s and the first half of the 1960s, the period of the long-boom, or 'the golden age', immortalised in Macmillan's words 'You've never had it so good'. Macmillan was right. The 1950s saw a fundamental transformation of working-class life in Britain and elsewhere, as full employment and mass production created the basis for mass consumption. Full employment also created the conditions for the end of deference and the gradual development of rising aspirations on the part of the working class. British capitalism during this period was able to satisfy the key components of the post-war historic bloc - capital, labour and the political classes. However, by the second half of the 1960s problems were developing.

The recovery of Germany and Japan, and their faster growth rates, together with the process of decolonisation and the end of Empire, led to intensifying international competition. Domestically, the prolonged period of full employment had changed the balance of forces between capital and labour in the labour market. At the same time, the balance of power between the ex-colonies and the industrialised capitalist countries had changed, partly due to political independence, partly because of the impact of rapid growth on the demand for primary commodities. The result was intensifying distributional conflict and an accelerating rate of inflation. In Britain, the weakest of the major capitalist economies, this was associated with a deepening balance of payments problem, which gave rise to the well-known phenomena of stop-go policies and stagflation.

As British capitalism ceased to be able to satisfy the key components of the post-war historic bloc, a period of social and political crisis developed. The first response was an attempt at modernisation, started under the Conservative government and continued by Labour when it assumed office in 1964. There were three main strands to this modernisation strategy: industrial policy, with the National Plan and the Industrial Reorganisation Corporation; industrial relations reform, with the Donovan Commission and In Place of Strife; and various attempts at Prices and Incomes Policy. In order to carry legitimacy and have a chance of success, these policies were in the main implemented through tripartite bodies, notably the National Economic Development Council, representing the major components of the historic bloc - the Confederation of British Industries, the Trades Union Congress and the Government.

In the event, the attempt at modernisation in Britain failed, for two main reasons. The economic policy foundations of the social democratic Keynesian welfare state were macroeconomic management, to maintain full employment and deal with the deepening balance of payments problem, and state provision of an efficient infrastructure. This provided the context for the operation of the economy at the micro level by private capital in pursuit of profit. Efficiency at the micro level was to be achieved by free competition between capitalists in factor and product markets and free collective bargaining between capital and labour in the labour market. Industrial policy in Britain failed because of the arms length relationship between government and capital, which meant that policy had to proceed with the consent of capital. The government was unwilling or unable to adopt policies with teeth. Industrial relations reform and incomes policies failed because of the resistance of labour to any encroachment on free collective bargaining. This stemmed from the economism of the labour movement, with its preoccupation with wages and conditions and its refusal to accept any responsibility for economic performance. It was this double failure of the modernisation strategy that ushered in the crisis of social democracy in Britain.

The conflict theory of inflation

The crisis made itself felt primarily in the accelerating rate of inflation (which by the summer of 1975 had reached an annual rate of 25 per cent), but also in an associated profits' squeeze. As Marx had long ago argued, the capitalist mode of production has its own inherent logic, its own law of motion, and central to that historically has been the trade cycle - the cycle of boom and slump, with its regular re-creation of mass unemployment, the industrial reserve army of labour. For Marx, mass unemployment was not some form of market failure but was functional for capitalism, as a means of keeping the working class in a subordinate position. Kalecki had already pointed out in 1943 that prolonged full employment would be a problem for capitalism, in that it would change the balance of power in the labour market and create inflationary pressure as workers pushed up money wages, and so it proved to be.[1] The effective suspension of the trade cycle meant that the regular creation of mass unemployment as a means of disciplining the working class, in the labour market and in the workplace, ceased to occur and inflation gradually gathered pace. In the debates on the left in the 1970s around the policies to be adopted in response to the crisis of social democracy, the causes of inflation, and hence the appropriate policies to deal with it, were hotly disputed. It was in this context that the conflict theory of inflation was developed, in opposition to the dominant monetarist theories that were becoming the conventional wisdom not only on the right but also on the left.

The essential structure of the conflict theory of inflation is as follows. The Keynesian social democratic welfare state created and sought to manage a situation in which there were the following dynamics: (i) in conditions of full employment workers could not be prevented from seeking real wage increases in excess of productivity growth; (ii) in a capitalist economy this objective could only be pursued by seeking to increase money wages; (iii) in oligopolistic markets capitalists were not prevented by competition from increasing money prices in order to maintain profits; and (iv) the state, in order to maintain full employment, increased the money supply to accommodate the higher wages and prices and allow the full employment level of output to continue to be sold at the higher prices. However, since total claims on output continued to exceed full employment output, the wage-price spiral was not halted but rather gradually accelerated.

In addition to this basic dynamic, which was more or less present in all the industrialised capitalist countries, albeit with significant variations, two other factors also made themselves felt in some countries, particularly in Britain. First, both workers and capitalists made demands on the state which required extra state expenditure, but resisted paying for it through higher taxes. Workers

---

1. M. Kalecki, 'Political Aspects of Full Employment', *Political Quarterly*, 14 4, 1943.

sought improvements in the welfare state services, the collective part of their real wage, while capitalists sought improvements in infrastructure and subsidies. Thus, as well as demands for increases in private consumption, workers sought increases in collective consumption, while capitalists sought increases in collective investment, as well as in private investment and their private consumption. However, neither workers nor capitalists were prepared to accept that increased state expenditure had to be financed, either by increased taxation, which they resisted, or by increases in the money supply, which is what happened. The wage-price spiral became a wage-public-expenditure-price-tax spiral.

The second additional factor at work resulted from the changed balance of power between the ex-colonial countries and the metropolitan capitalist countries. As continuous economic growth caused demand for primary commodities to outstrip supply, the primary commodity producing countries could not be prevented from increasing their prices and shifting the terms of trade in their favour, thus increasing the real price of their commodities. This resulted in an increase in import prices in the metropolitan capitalist countries which meant there was less real income available for domestic use, thus exacerbating the conflict over the distribution of full-employment real national income. The wage-public-expenditure-price-tax spiral now included increasing import prices as well as domestic prices. The most dramatic example of this process was, of course, the succession of oil price increases in the 1970s.[2]

Given the dominance of monetarist theories of inflation, it is important to realise that the money supply did undoubtedly increase during this period. However, this increase was not the underlying cause of the great inflation of the 1970s. The increase in the money supply was itself a consequence of the struggle between capital and labour over the division of full employment output. In the context of that struggle, in which workers increased money wages in order to obtain a larger share of output, and capitalists increased prices in order to prevent this, full employment output could only be bought at the higher prices if the money supply was increased. The increase

---

2. For a fuller discussion of the conflict theory of inflation, see P. Devine, 'Inflation and Marxist Theory', *Marxism Today*, March 1974; and 'The "Conflict Theory of Inflation" Revisited', in J. Toporowski (ed), *Political Economy and the New Capitalism*, Routledge, London 2003.

in the money supply was thus a necessary outcome of the commitment to full employment. Only when that commitment had been abandoned at the end of the 1970s, did it became possible to seek to contain the money supply. A restrictive policy towards the money supply is merely a means of disciplining labour through the acceptance of mass unemployment if workers do not restrain their demands for a larger, or in some circumstances even the same, share of real output. The Bundesbank's overriding objective of controlling inflation, subsequently imposed on the European Central Bank, and New Labour's decision to give the Bank of England 'independence' in pursuit of a government imposed low inflation target, both followed from the political decision that inflation was more of a problem than unemployment. If unemployment was the only way of disciplining the workforce, so be it. Of course, for this policy to be possible a fundamental change in the post-war balance of forces was necessary. It is the achievement of this that has been the historic mission of the new right's neoliberalism since the late 1970s.[3]

The 1970s: the end of social democracy

By 1970 the basis of the post-war consensus had gone. Capitalism had begun to seize up as the Keynesian welfare state, with its full employment, rising aspirations, and the ability of the labour movement to pursue them, increasingly closed off the sources of renewal within the capitalist mode of production - the scrapping of the least efficient capital equipment during a slump and the reduction of wages as a result of mass unemployment. At the same time, the recovery of Germany and Japan and the dynamic of capitalist development were producing an increasingly integrated global economy, with the consequence that competition between capitals was intensifying, and by 1973 the Bretton Woods system of fixed exchange rates had collapsed. In this historical conjuncture, two alternative post-social democracy trajectories presented themselves: a move in the direction of economic democracy, building on the gains of the long-boom, as a transitional stage towards socialism; or a move to neoliberalism, reversing the post-1945 gains.

The radical alternative economic strategy developed in the 1970s was an

---

3. The lower rates of growth associated with higher unemployment also had the incidental effect of weakening the demand for primary commodities, thus shifting the terms of trade against the commodity producing countries.

attempt to provide a framework for the former. It recognised that inflation, in the conditions of post-1945 capitalism, was the result of distributional conflict between classes and groups which were sufficiently powerful that they could not be prevented from claiming a larger share of real output, necessarily at the expense of other classes or groups, but were not powerful enough to impose their claims on others. It argued for the acceptance of prices and incomes policies in order to control inflation, but on conditions. If workers were to accept real income increases that remained in line with productivity increases, two things were necessary. First, the initial distribution between wages and profits had to be agreed - it could not be assumed that the existing distribution was acceptable as a starting point. Second, since real wage increases would then depend on productivity increases, labour had to be involved in the decisions that determined the rate of increase of productivity - decisions about investment and innovation. Thus, the corollary of accepting prices and incomes policies was encroachment on managerial prerogatives by moving towards industrial democracy, planning agreements and eventually increased social ownership.

'full-blown neoliberal Thatcherism fundamentally reversed the shift in favour of labour that had emerged from the second world war'

This radical strategy was not only opposed by capital and its representatives, but also by an unholy alliance of on the one hand the right in the Labour Party and trade unions, and on the other the old left steeped in economistic labourism. The Communist Party and Labour militants successfully used their influence in the trade union and shop stewards movements to defend free collective bargaining and oppose incomes policies. The result was the acceleration of inflation to its high point of 25 per cent in the summer of 1975. There was, of course, a minority left presence in the Labour government of the time, most notably Benn at the Ministry of Technology, which advocated aspects of the alternative strategy, in particular planning agreements. However, the left, including supporters of the radical alternative economic strategy, still thought in terms primarily of the national economy, advocating import and exchange controls to contain the balance of payments problem and opposing the European Common Market. If there was a single moment symbolising the defeat of the left's bid for power and the end of any prospect, however slight, of the radical alternative economic strategy being adopted, it was the failure of the 'No' campaign in the 1975 referendum on whether Britain should stay in the Common Market, which was rapidly followed by the demotion of Benn.

Of course, the prospect of the radical alternative economic strategy ever having been adopted was indeed slight. For this to have happened, the organised labour movement would have had to have developed a Gramscian hegemonic consciousness and strategy for the creation of a new historic bloc around a project of national democratic renewal and advance. A progressive hegemonic consciousness would have been one that aspired to the leadership of the society as a whole, rising above the defensive consciousness and sectional interests of the working class under capitalism and taking a view of how policies to meet the pressing needs of all the social classes and groups in the new conjuncture could be articulated around a transformatory project and discourse. It was precisely this that the economism of the trade unions and the reformist formation of the Labour Party precluded.

The outcome was that the second alternative post-social democracy trajectory, the turn to neoliberalism, was all that remained. After the symbolic defeat of the left in the 1975 referendum, militant labourism continued to resist this solution, culminating in the 1978/9 'winter of discontent', but to no avail. The Labour government abandoned the commitment to full employment and replaced it with the control of inflation as the priority economic objective. Unemployment started to rise. The scene was set for the 1980s era of full-blown neoliberal Thatcherism which decisively destroyed militant labourism and fundamentally reversed the shift in the balance of forces in favour of labour that had emerged from the second world war.

The dark ages: the 1980s and 1990s

Although most closely associated with the Thatcher era, neoliberalism did not suddenly emerge from nowhere. Thatcherism had been prepared for over a long period by a growing number of right-wing think tanks influenced above all by the work of Hayek, notably in the early years the Institute of Economic Affairs. This ideological offensive focused around the two principal components of Hayek's thought: the danger to freedom posed by discretionary state activity; and the role of markets as the institution best suited to guaranteeing individual freedom. This was a radical right alternative vision to the paternalism of the post-second world war social democratic welfare state. It had an increasing resonance with people's rising aspirations for more control over their lives, and for more responsive services from the welfare state and the nationalised utilities, as real incomes rose and memories of the inter-war period faded. However, it sought to articulate these aspirations within a hegemonic neoliberal individualism, rather than realise them through a turn to radical economic, social and political democracy.

In the 1970s and early 1980s British politics could be seen as being characterised by two main dimensions - left-right and radical-conservative. The post-war social democratic consensus was between the conservative left and right. The crisis of social democracy meant that that consensus was no longer viable. Radical change was required. The radical alternative economic strategy was the attempt of a minority on the left to respond to this challenge and hegemonise people's rising aspirations within a left perspective by articulating them in a society-wide project of deepening democracy. As we have seen, this attempt was opposed by the conservative Labour right and the equally conservative economistic militant left. Of course, the radical alternative economic strategy had its weaknesses: a residual statism and productivism; insufficient awareness of the issues raised by the new social movements - feminist, anti-racist and environmental; and an overly narrow focus on the national economy. Nevertheless, it was a heroic effort and its failure left the field wide open for the neoliberal radical right.[4]

The first half of the 1980s saw the effective destruction of militant labourism, culminating in the defeat of the last great miners' strike of 1984-85. Anti-trade union legislation transformed the character of the trade union movement from a defender of workers' interests in the labour market and the workplace into a provider of personal services to its members. Trade union membership fell dramatically, partly as a result of the new legislation, but also because of the process of deindustrialisation underway, which affected disproportionately the more densely unionised industries. Unemployment, which had averaged 3.8 per cent during the 1970s - already double the rate of the 1960s - rose to an average of 9.6 per cent in the 1980s.

---

4. For a discussion of the strategy's weaknesses, see S. Aaronovitch, 'The Alternative Economic Strategy: Goodbye to All That?', *Marxism Today*, 30 2, 1986.

Correspondingly, inflation, which had averaged 13.9 per cent in the 1970s, fell to an average of 6.4 per cent in the 1980s.[5] Incomes policies having failed in the 1970s, the 1980s saw the recreation of mass unemployment as a means of disciplining labour. This was also central to creating the conditions for the process of replacing collective consciousness and solidarity with an individual consciousness in which people think of themselves primarily as individual workers and consumers, not as citizens.

In addition to policies that directly changed the balance of forces in society, there were also policies to provide incentives to embrace the emerging new individualistic common sense of the age. Although privatisation through capital market flotations and top-management buy-outs transferred public property to the private sector at knock-down prices, resulting in scandalous capital gains, it also sought to create the illusion of a people's capitalism by significantly increasing the proportion of the population that owned shares. Of course, this occurred at the same time as the concentration of share ownership in the largest holdings continued to increase, but it nevertheless had an ideological effect. Similarly, the introduction of the right of tenants to buy their council houses also contributed to the ideology of a property owning democracy.

It took a long time to roll back the historic gains of labour that underlay the post-war consensus and the era of social democracy, and even today there are significant differences in the extent to which this has occurred in different countries. In Britain it was not until the early 1990s that the changed balance of forces and the lowering of expectations, with a corresponding reduction in the rate of inflation, were consolidated. By the mid-1990s the inflation rate had fallen from the 1980s average of 6.4 per cent to between 2 per cent and 3 per cent, and it has remained at this level ever since. Unemployment fell from an average of 9.6 per cent in the 1980s to an average of 7.9 per cent in the 1990s and has been around 5 per cent since 2001, without this resulting in an increase in inflation.

This last period of relatively low unemployment and low inflation shows that it is a mistake to argue, as some have suggested, that there is an inverse relation between unemployment and inflation, irrespective of the period concerned. This relationship did hold during the long boom in the era of social

---

5. All figures in this article are taken from the European Commission's *European Economy: Annual Report for 2004*, Directorate-General for Economic and Financial Affairs, Brussels 2004.

democracy, although the variations were small. However, the changed balance of forces in the new era of neoliberalism, and the associated lowering of aspirations, means that the relationship no longer holds, although it is worth remembering that unemployment at around 5 per cent is still significantly higher than the 1960s average of 1.7 per cent and the 1970s average of 3.8 per cent. This is a salutary reminder of the power of ideology, which, when it becomes the common sense of the age, acts as a material force in society, setting limits to what is thought possible and shaping behaviour.

O f course, the mass unemployment that re-emerged in Britain during the 1980s and first half of the 1990s, and still persists today in much of Continental Europe, was not the only new factor contributing to the changed balance of forces underpinning neoliberalism. Three other major developments have to be taken into account. First, there has been a big increase in global competition. The ability of capitalists to increase prices in the face of rising wages and import prices is heavily dependent on the degree of competition between them. The process of globalisation, encouraged by the national governments of the leading capitalist countries and animated by the multinationals, has to a large extent undermined the old oligopolistic relationship between capitals within the national economy, and this has greatly increased the intensity of competition worldwide. Second, the change in the balance of power brought about by decolonisation has been undermined by the neoliberal policies imposed on the third world by the IMF, World Bank and World Trade Organisation, although there are now signs of growing opposition to the new US imperialism. Finally, the re-emergence of mass unemployment and the dominance of US-driven policies of privatisation and deregulation were at least in part made possible by the weakening and then collapse of the Soviet Union and its allies, which left the US as the sole superpower for the time being and capitalism as the only game in town.

The role of New Labour: a future for social democracy?

The 1980s were the decade in which the historic bloc underpinning the post war-consensus was decisively destroyed, but this process was not without its costs, and this resulted in growing opposition. The increasing unpopularity of Thatcher with the electorate culminated in the Conservative Party palace coup in 1990 which replaced her with Major. However, despite his subsequent unexpected 1992 election victory, Major can be seen as a transitional figure and, by 1997, after eighteen years of Tory rule, the country had had enough. What can be said about the role of New Labour in the new context? To what extent can it be seen as providing a renewed impetus to social democracy?

Even though New Labour assumed office as the principal beneficiary of a partial rejection of policies associated with neoliberalism, it was from the start fully committed to the neoliberal agenda that Thatcherism had gone a long way to making the new common sense of the age. Far from seeking to overturn this new commonsense, New Labour embarked on an altogether different project. While Thatcherism had destroyed the old historic bloc and created the basis for a new neoliberal era, it had not yet succeeded in creating a new historic bloc in which neoliberal principles and policies became the generally accepted ideological cement holding it together. This was to become the historic mission of New Labour.[6]

Economically, New Labour has pursued a relentless neoliberal free market strategy, seeking to create and consolidate a corporate business-friendly domestic and global environment. However, it is in relation to the welfare state that the distinctive character of New Labour's neoliberalism is apparent. After the initial period in which it accepted the public expenditure plans of the Conservatives, New Labour has significantly increased public expenditure, but on strict conditions, conditions it has sought to impose through an unremitting centralisation of power, the proliferation of unaccountable charitable or not-for-profit agencies, and the sidelining of local government.

The organising principle of the 'modernising reforms' on which New Labour has insisted as the price for increased public expenditure has been the transformation of the public sector from being operated on the basis of public service to being operated on the basis of market principles and 'value for money'. It is premised on the ideology that the private sector and business people are more efficient than the public sector and public servants. Patients, students, passengers, clients and citizens have been redefined as consumers. Public servants have been replaced by business people, managers of marketised state and non-state agencies and social entrepreneurs. The spin rationalising all this has been ending the power of bureaucracy and vested professional interests,

---

6. See, S. Hall, 'New Labour's Double-Shuffle', *Soundings* 24.

transferring power from producers to consumers, and giving people control over their lives by providing choice. This was started by Thatcherism but has been generalised and universalised by New Labour and given a material basis by the increased public expenditure.

Freedom from the paternalistic 'nanny state', assuming personal responsibility for one's own life through the exercise of market choice, has also been the smokescreen under which the role of the state has been transformed from that of collective provision and solidarity on behalf of society as a whole, of people as citizens, into that of 'helping people to help themselves'. Policies to encourage those not working back into the labour force have resulted in some reduction in poverty, especially child poverty. However, this has coexisted with an increase in inequality as corporate directors have also helped themselves, irrespective of corporate success, to massive bonuses, capital gains and golden handshakes. What remains of the citizen-based solidaristic principle is confined to the provision of a safety net for those who cannot be brought to fend for themselves. Thus, New Labour is consciously creating a two-tier system, in which those who can, look after themselves, and those who can't, or won't, receive charity provided by a reluctant and disapproving state.

Despite the continuing resistance to New Labour's strategy of economic neoliberalism and the neoliberal marketisation of the state, it would be a mistake to underestimate the potential attractiveness of aspects of this strategy. The statism, paternalism, social engineering, inefficiency and prioritisation of producer over consumer interests associated with reformist social democracy all proved increasingly unpopular. The operation of representative democracy, with voters asked to choose a government at periodic intervals and then let it get on with deciding policy and implementing it, in the period of consensus when the outcome made less and less difference, led to disillusionment with the political process and falling turnout at elections. People sensed that radical change was needed. The reason why the 1970s are so crucial for an understanding of the present situation is that they were the decade in which the dynamic for necessary change was hegemonised by the neoliberal agenda. This does not mean that change was not necessary. The alternative to New Labour's neoliberal marketisation of all aspects life cannot be a return to Old Labour's paternalistic social democracy. It must instead be a move towards radical democratisation.

The new millennium: insights from the political economy of the past

Politics in the New Millennium is characterised by the overwhelming dominance of the neoliberal agenda. There are, as always, movements of résistance and dreams of another world being possible. However, until a forward-looking project of radical democratic renewal and reconstruction is developed, these will not become a coherent force, sustained in the long run, for fundamental change. The situation confronting the planet could hardly be more threatening - global capitalism is proving increasingly incompatible with social justice, ecological sustainability, and the rule of law, nationally and internationally. The principal insight to be drawn from the political economy of the 1970s and after is the need for a historical perspective and a hegemonic strategy. As we have seen, Thatcherism did not emerge from nowhere. Unlike New Labour, it did not seek to adapt to and consolidate an existing agenda. It was carefully prepared for and represented a conscious attempt to change the agenda, to alter the common sense of the age. It was an immensely successful hegemonic strategy.

Policies are, of course, essential, but they are not enough. They need to be shaped in relation to the social forces existing and developing in society with a view to reconfiguring them in a transformatory way, so that these forces come together to form a new historic bloc articulated around a radical democratic agenda for civil society, the state and the economy. The organising principles of such a bloc might be: democratisation not marketisation; citizens not consumers; solidarity not selfishness; participation not alienation; ecological sustainability and social justice. There is no shortage of social forces, overlapping and intersecting, that might potentially come together to constitute such a new historic bloc. What is missing, however, in this age of public historical amnesia, is a collective consciousness of the lessons to be drawn from the past half century and the confidence that with strategic vision another world really is possible.[7]

A hegemonic strategy for today must be based on radical participatory democracy. Disenchantment with conventional representative politics coexists

---

7. For a survey of left policies since the 1970s, see N. Thompson, *Left in the Wilderness: The Political Economy of British Democratic Socialism Since 1979*, Acumen, Chesham 2002.

with endless examples of people seeking control over their lives in relation to issues that affect them directly or that they care passionately about. Movements against environmental degradation and for a better quality of life are to be found among the poor of the third world as much as among the more affluent in the industrialised world.[8] It is increasingly evident that global ecological sustainability and global social justice are necessary conditions for each other - and equally evident that neither is possible within a global capitalist system that generates inequality and is driven by a dynamic of continuous economic expansion. The changes required to achieve a better quality of life for all are so great that they can only be realised through a participatory process seeking negotiated consensus. The development of a hegemonic strategy around this perspective requires the coming together of the left and green movements, the two social forces with an interest in the profound transformations that are necessary.

---

8. See J. Martinez-Alier, *The Environmentalism of the Poor: A Study of Ecological Conflicts and Valuation*, Edward Elgar, Cheltenham 2002.

Gramsci in history seminar

Wednesday 19 July 2006
University of East Anglia, Norwich, UK

Speakers include Tom Nairn, Ann Showstack Sassoon, David Forgacs, David Purdy, Pat Devine, Mike Prior, Gino Bedaro, Giuseppe Vatalaro

Sessions include Gramsci now; Gramsci and New Labour; The phases of British Gramscism; Gramscian economics in the 1970s; Gramsci and Fascism; Gramsci, social movements and the third world; Gramsci and violence.

Plus two further themes to be decided (suggestions welcome!)

There is a fee of £25 (£10 for students and unwaged) to cover costs.

Inquiries, applications, offers of papers etc: andrew.pearmain@ntlworld.com

Restating a politics of 'the public'

Janet Newman

Janet Newman *looks at contemporary struggles about the meaning of 'the public'.*

Nearly a decade ago Maureen Mackintosh, introducing a special issue of *Soundings* on 'The Public Good' (Issue 4, 1996), commented that 'we seem to have lost confidence in our ability to construct a public sphere which promotes the public good'. While people continued to pursue efforts to sustain and nurture public services, public speech and public action, they did so 'against a tide of malevolent divisiveness which has its roots in public policy'. The debates on how notions of the public and publicness are being remade in contemporary politics and culture have continued in *Soundings* and elsewhere. Yet I remain deeply concerned about the difficulty of speaking the language of public and publicness in contemporary discourse. Despite the focus by all of the main political parties on public services - this is one of the areas in which any notion of 'clear blue water' between Labour and Conservative appears elusive - the publicness of those services is viewed as somehow outdated, part of the old world of the universal welfare state rather than the new world of flexibility, modernity and consumerism.

But this is not to say that we can simply look back regretfully (and nostalgically) at a vanishing social democratic public sphere. Those once simple equations of publicness and state can no longer hold, especially if we take account of the critiques of the social democratic state that have emerged from a succession of social movements over the last three decades. Given the new forms of politics that these produced, how can we now understand the shifting configurations of 'the public', while at the same time attempting to defend it from the onslaughts of neo-liberalism?

In this article I want to address a key dilemma - a dilemma that comes out of my own experience of crossing and re-crossing the boundary between academic work and what those outside the academy like to call 'the real world'. As an academic I am aware of a range of writings from cultural theorists - Raymond Williams, Michael Warner, Clive Barnett - that have problematised the idea of a simple duality between public and private; and of the work of feminist scholars - Ruth Lister, Ann Phillips, Iris Marion Young - who have pointed to the structural exclusions from the public domain of citizenship and the limitations of its democratic institutions. Indeed the language of public domain, public sphere, public realm, all imply a rather spatial metaphor that fails to capture the mobile, elusive and shifting character of publicness. However I also remain someone who is closely engaged with the fortunes of the public sector, of those who work in it and those who benefit from it (or not) - and as such I want to argue that the publicness of public institutions and public discourse is something to be struggled over.

In what follows I begin by delineating some of the terrains in which the contemporary politics of the public is indeed being struggled over. Rather than a single dynamic - based around a state/market binary - I argue that a number of different dynamics are at stake here. I then go on to trace how these different dynamics inform contemporary struggles around the remaking of public policy, public services and public institutions under New Labour. Finally I suggest ways in which it might be possible to work towards restating a politics of publicness. To do so, I argue, it is important to go beyond social democratic conceptions of the public sphere.

The politics of the public

This is a moment at which struggles over what is and what is not a public matter are intensifying. They encompass struggles over security with the dismantling of protections of privacy following 9/11 and the emergence of a new politics of fear; struggles over the environment, and the private abuse of global resources; struggles around sexuality, including how far the state may regulate or intervene into the private, what sexualities are publicly recognised and what practices may occupy public space; struggles over issues of reproduction following challenges to the personal integrity of the body through advances in genetic engineering (and indeed the ownership of those technologies); and even struggles over that most personal moment, death, with conflicts about the right to die increasingly hitting the headlines and with debates about who can decide to terminate life support systems intensifying. Furthermore, in the UK the question of whether financial provision for income in old age is a matter for the state, for employers or personal prudentialism is moving to the centre of the political agenda, while the extent of the role of the market in the provision of higher education, healthcare and social care will continue to be contested.

Now across those struggles we can trace a lot of confusions in the definitions used. Privacy may be viewed as a negative freedom from incursions of the state; a private domain of domestic and personal life; or the privacy of the consumer making individualised choices in the marketplace rather than subscribing to collective provision of public services. Publicness may denote the Habermasean public sphere of communicative rationality and democratic engagement; or could mean the public sector, publicly owned resources, public space, public values and so on. But the shifting boundary between public, private and personal is not just a matter of definitional nicety - it is the focus of new governmental processes through which the boundaries are reordered, and of active contestation, border skirmishes and infringements. I want to offer four quick examples of this reworking of public and private, each involving different forms of slippage between political, economic and moral inflections.

The first concerns the 2005 legislation on civil partnerships, enabling gay and lesbian couples a measure of public legitimacy. This has been the result of a long struggle, and the struggle is by no means over. The example shows how public legitimacy for private relationships is informed by changing cultural norms, and how such norms may be inscribed and institutionalised in legislation. But it also opens out questions about the boundary between public and private space, and what kinds of sexualities may - and may not - be performed publicly. For gay and lesbian couples the public performance of sexual identity is still heavily circumscribed, especially outside 'metropolitan' public space. And the apparent liberalisation in one area is offset by deepening concerns about the loss of earlier gains in others. Domestic violence, abortion, and reproduction - issues that women struggled to get on the public agenda in the nineteenth and twentieth centuries - are in the twenty-first the focus of efforts by the moral right within a new politics of the personal, which seeks to reassert patriarchal authority and a conservative moral agenda. Such issues highlight not only the contested boundary of the personal and the public, but also that between moral and political inflections of gender and sexuality. And, as the impact of the infamous Section 28 (part of the Local Government Act of 1988, banning the 'promotion' of homosexuality in schools, youth organisations and other public institutions) showed, morality and politics can often form an unhappy conjunction in the framing of public policy.

My second example also relates to the personal/public boundary, eliding the distinction between personal belief and public culture. This has long been a site of historical tensions between church and state, and tensions have taken new forms in the context of the importance of 'faith' issues in defining and delimiting (and often essentialising) notions of multiculturalism. This could be seen in the controversy over Birmingham Repertory Theatre's production of *Bhezti* in 2004, as part of a series designed to reach out to black and other minority ethnic publics. Despite attempts by the theatre to engage in extensive consultation, this play drew vocal protests from what the press termed the local Sikh community. Now the notion of an integrated, univocal Sikh community is of course deeply problematic. It masks differences of gender and generation, differences that were very significant here since the play depicted incidents of domestic violence against women in a holy Sikh place. Not only did this raise issues of how the boundary between public and personal is culturally contested; it also highlighted the question of who can speak about - and for - communities; who has a public voice; and whose voices are silenced. This is enormously important in the context of current policies designed to extend and enhance public participation in the shaping of policy, and in the delivery of services. The example also suggests ways in which public space - inside the theatre as well as in the square outside where the demonstrations took place - is differently inhabited and experienced; and what happens when the borders of such spaces are contested.

My third example is the move towards new strategies for governing the social that render more of the personal available for public scrutiny and public intervention. Far from seeing the demise of the authoritarian paternalism of the welfare state, we are now seeing its extension in a range of policies that address how we should live our lives. These include policies on anti-social behaviour that attempt to make parents responsible for the behaviour of their children; the 'welfare to work' policies that include the need for unemployed people to work to a personal development plan to re-equip them for the workplace; policies linked to the new 'personal prudentialism' that is, in part, supposed to solve the problem of the looming pensions crisis, and many others. Two initiatives from within the health service are particularly noteworthy here. The first is the new willingness of some health authorities and trusts to be explicit in their prioritisation of treatment for patients who conform to particular norms (a previously informal and unacknowledged practice). For example the East Anglia NHS Trust announced in December 2005 that patients who were seriously obese may be denied hip or knee replacements in an attempt to stave off the Trust's debts. The National Institute for Clinical Excellence picked up this issue in a report emphasising the importance of cost effectiveness in judgements about how far 'self inflicted' medical conditions such as smoking might have an impact on the type of treatments given. This 'publicises', in a debate about medical judgements, decisions that were previously within the province of informal rationing by individual clinicians. The second initiative is the 'expert patient' scheme, through which patients with long standing illnesses are given training in how to manage their own treatment more effectively. This is an interesting conjuncture of two different imperatives: the professional drive towards patient involvement and empowerment in order to secure better health outcomes, and a more resource-driven imperative to reduce pressure on GP surgeries and to shift the burden of costs from expensive interventions (especially hospital admissions) towards lower cost preventative work. Both of these examples suggest the significance of 'responsibilisation' as a way of redrawing the boundary between public services and private responsibility, a particularly significant dimension of the retreat from the social democratic welfare state. But both also suggest ways in which the publicness of public services is a site of ongoing strain.

My final example concerns what is probably the dominant strategy for remaking the public - its abandonment in the face of marketisation and privatisation - but also the moments that apparently challenge this dominance. In the last year or so we have seen a retreat by the Secretary of State for Health on a proposed policy to introduce markets into community health services, and significant backbench parliamentary resistance to the Education Bill. One very high profile challenge to the government was Jamie Oliver's crusade to improve school dinners. This condensed in one campaign both the impact on the public sector of heroic images from the worlds of commerce and celebrity, and the importance of the media in shaping and reshaping ideas of what is and is not a public matter. After some initial success - in securing the promise of more funds from government to improve school meals - it subsequently emerged that new schools built under the private finance initiative could make very few changes, because they were locked into 25-year contracts, while other schools would have to pay significant financial penalties to opt out of long running contracts with private catering companies. The Turkey Twizzler lives on.

Across these different stories - the legalisation of civil partnerships, the Sikh protest, 'responsible' or 'expert patients', and the Jamie Oliver campaign - I have sketched out a number of different dynamics at stake in the politics of remaking the public. These can be summarised as:

♦ *going to market* - the increasing use of the market for the provision of public goods and the potential displacement of collective identifications and allegiances that this produces

♦ *obscuring the public* - the turn to public/private partnerships, contracting and network forms of co-ordination, all of which obscure the boundaries between state, market and civil society

♦ *publicising the personal* - new governmental strategies of responsibilisation and more direct forms of intervention into how we live our personal lives

♦ *contesting publicness* - struggles over spaces and around acts of publicness in the context of multi-cultural and differentiated societies.

In what follows I want to trace ways in which these contradictions are played out in the reform and modernisation of public services, beginning with the strategy of 'going to market'.

Going to market

The contracting out of public services is a process that has challenged the clarity of the boundary between public and private: that is, not only has it externalised some services, it has also brought the logic of the market deep inside those that remained public. This is a process that has continued with later initiatives - best value, purchaser/provider splits, public/private partnerships, and so on. Each is predicated on a search for economy and efficiency, which in theory is to be balanced by a requirement that accountability should be inscribed in the new mechanisms of contract, and by the proliferation of audit and other regulatory measures (for a discussion of audit culture see Mike Rustin in *Soundings* 26). However concepts such as economy and efficiency - and indeed accountability - have to be understood as social constructs whose meaning is struggled over in the process of tendering and contracting. The processes of social construction and meaning-making have very significant consequences, not only for the distribution of resources between the public and private sectors, but also for the identities of those engaged in the transformation of the public sector. This applies both to those on the inside (the transformation of bureaucrats and professionals into managers) and on the outside (bringing commercial, third sector and community organisations into new forms of governmental power through the contracting process).

The dynamics of remaking the public takes place across a field of structured inequalities. For example, the school meals campaign included a call for better pay for dinner ladies so that they could have time to cook freshly prepared food, as opposed to composing pre-packaged meals from suppliers. Dinner ladies are of course an example of the kinds of workers that moved from public to private sector in the marketising reforms of the 1980s and 1990s. During this process the wages and conditions of such workers suffered, as did the quality of their work, and their capacity to deliver public value - whether this is defined in terms of healthy children, clean hospitals or quality of life for those in need of long-term care. This opens out a different kind of politics of the public, raising issues about who is employed in what conditions, as well as what kinds of work are deemed to be a public or collective responsibility. And it is a very gendered politics. The welfare state can be viewed as making public - and institutionalising - women's domestic and emotional labour. Its modernisation involves gender dynamics in a number of ways. The shifting of responsibility from the public to the personal sphere (where it still tends to be women who pick up responsibility for forms of welfare that have been privatised onto individuals and families) is taking place at the same time that women are being encouraged to be full worker citizens through various welfare to work schemes - as well as being expected to play a role as active citizens in the new policies on community and service-user participation. The gaps opened up in these contradictory imperatives are filled in part by the further stretching of the elasticity of women's labour, and in part through the development of a new service economy of domestic and personal services - an economy peopled by migrant labour. It is workers in this marginal economy of low paid, flexible and vulnerable employment that experience most acutely the stresses created by the withdrawal of the state; such workers are picking up responsibility for forms of welfare that have been privatised onto individuals and families, as well as experiencing successive waves of intensification in their own paid work.

Obscuring the public

The dynamics of going to market serves to residualise the public in its instantiation in a public sector, but it also has the effect of obscuring the public/ private boundary so that it becomes more difficult to debate and contest what is and is not a public matter. Geoff Andrews (*Soundings* 22, 2003) argues that 'a key component of the Third Way of managing public services is the idea that forms of ownership are no longer important: that it is how things are delivered that counts'. This assumption is clearly one that opens up the state to more and more extensive processes of marketisation. However I want to argue that in New Labour's struggle for legitimacy - in what Johnson and Steinberg term its 'war of persuasion' - the *appearance* of publicness is crucial.[1] This takes different forms in different services and has contradictory effects. In health, the idea of the NHS as a public institution is critical to Labour's political platform; however it is in health that the ethos of consumerism has perhaps been most extensively applied, with commercial treatment centres enabling Health Authorities to offer their 'customers' shorter waiting times,

---

1. R. Johnson and D. Steinberg (eds), *Blairism and the War of Persuasion: Labour's Passive Revolution*. Lawrence and Wishart 2004.

as well as some (albeit highly constrained) 'choice' of provider. In education the use of PFI to build new schools has gone relatively unmarked, while the issue of commercial sponsorship of books, computers and other resources has been hotly contested. At the same time, the rise in MRSA infection rates in hospitals, and the decline in the quality of school meals, have been deemed public matters that require government intervention. However the privatisation of cleaning and catering services under the Tories that, arguably, lies at the root of such problems has not been put on the public or political agenda. What we can see here is the residualisation of the public in its institutional embodiment in the state, but taking place at the same time as its augmentation in political discourse.

To understand these contradictions we need to distinguish between different kinds of relationship between the public and the state, private business and the market: 'If they are all lumped together and the term "privatisation" used to inspire loathing, rather than understanding, the effect will be to close debate that needs to be stimulated' (Brendan Martin in *Soundings* 28). Rather than a single logic - privatisation - the residualisation of the public rests on multiple logics in a complex re-making of forms and relationships of power. However, this very multiplicity and complexity - contracts interwoven inside contracts, multiple forms of partnership, the explosion of regulatory and audit bodies, and more recently the turn to new collaborative relationships with citizens themselves - serves to mask where the publicness of public services or the public interest is now to be found.

This tendency is exacerbated by the rise of managerialism as the dominant logic of co-ordination. In *The Managerial State*, John Clarke and I traced how the dispersal of state power under Thatcherism was only possible because of the significance of managerialism as a co-ordinating rationality, one that inscribed new logics of decision-making, reshaping regimes of power across the public sector.[2] These logics and rationalities came to the centre of government with New Labour, permeating its programme of modernisation and introducing a strongly managerial style of politics itself. It is not my intention here to try and retrace the extensive analyses of New Labour that

---

2. J. Clarke and J. Newman, *The Managerial State: power, politics and ideology in the remaking of social welfare*, Sage 1997.

have taken place in *Soundings* and elsewhere over the last decade; but I do want to highlight the importance of looking at the ways in which the tensions at the core of the Third Way were played out in public policy and in Labour's modernisation agenda.[3]

Publicising the personal: making up managers

There are of course many ways in which contemporary governance strategies involve an attempt to manage the person: encouraging citizens to take greater responsibility for their own health; to be active citizens in self-governed communities; to manage their own disruptive or truanting children more effectively, and so on. Something that has received rather less attention is the opening up of public service actors to new strategies of self management and self regulation. The tensions in New Labour's programme of modernisation - between the centralisation of power and increasingly managerial style of governance on the one hand, and the increasing emphasis on local involvement and empowerment on the other - has created spaces that allow the possibility of agency, on the part of state and non state actors. This then raises the question of who public service managers think they are: managerial roles and identities are discursively constituted. Thus one of the ways in which the boundary between personal and public is remade through governmental strategies is this opening up of the personal commitments, allegiances and linguistic resources of professionals and administrators to new governmental strategies. Workers in and beyond the state have to undertake extensive performative work when taking on a managerial persona and adopting managerialism as a legitimating discourse.[4]

This mention of performativity conveys, I hope, the sense that new discourses - however powerful - are not necessarily successful in constituting new subjectivities: it is crucial to go beyond the 'discovery' of discourse and analysis of its logics in order to explore ways in which new discourses are articulated with others in complex re-workings of identity and social practice. My work with senior civil servants, local government workers, professionals in health, probation, social care and those working in the voluntary sector over

3. See J. Newman, *Modernising Governance: New Labour, Policy and Society,* Sage 2001.
4. J. Clarke, 'Performing for the public: doubt, desire and the evaluation of public services', in P. du Gay (ed), *The Values of Bureaucracy,* Oxford University Press 2005.

the last two decades has taught me the importance of identifying what happens in the spaces created when traditional commitments and affiliations - to local communities, to service users, to staff - encounter new managerial ideologies of delegation and empowerment. Public service professionals and managers are well able to inflect older forms of politics - drawn from feminism, community activism, trades unionism - with new political rationalities, or to articulate professional values - based on vocabularies of need or of user empowerment - with new discourses of consumerism and choice.[5]

I don't want to romanticise public service professionals and managers as defenders of publicness - it is, after all, through their agency that governmental power is enacted and managerial power embedded. But I do want to highlight their role in managing the contradictory logics of reform - and the importance of studying how they negotiate the tension between business accountability and a wider sense of cultural or ethical responsibility.[6] And I want to suggest that such questions are becoming more important as the generation who grew up and began working in the Thatcher years come through into senior management and policy roles.

Contesting publics

One of the features of contemporary developments in public policy is the turn to consumerism. In a recent research project at the Open University - 'Creating citizen-consumers: changing relationships and identifications' - we studied the ways in which policy documents have attempted to resolve a number of contradictions facing New Labour; in particular we looked at ways in which they sought to reconcile a social democratic language of equality with the discourse of flexibility, responsiveness and choice.[7] In this process the idea of a solidaristic public, and its instantiation in national institutions such as the NHS, is dismantled in favour of a shallow and individualised conception of personal choice. This, as Blair himself has indicated, was intended to bind the middle class into continued support for public services, rather than to produce an

---

5. J. Newman, 'Network governance, transformational leadership and the micro politics of public service change', *Sociology*, October 2005.
6. J. Newman, 'Constructing accountability: network governance and managerial agency', *Public Policy and Administration*, 19, 4, 2004.
7. www.open-university/socialsciences/citizenconsumers

assault on the idea of a publicly provided and publicly funded NHS. However the effects are rather different when combined with the idea of 'money following patients', in an increasingly competitive field in which the private sector is invited to play a more and more significant role. We can, then, see a double process of transformation, in which the idea of a solidaristic public is being dismantled at the same time as the national institution that in part sustained it is being fragmented (through decentralisation to quasi independent foundation hospitals as well as through increasing reliance on market mechanisms and competition).

However, alongside this erosion of national solidarities we can see an increasing governmental concern with 'community' and 'neighbourhood' as a new locus for strategies of social inclusion. An array of policies - especially from the Home Office - have focused on the importance of 'active communities', and indeed 'faith communities', as both the foundation of and expression of 'modern' citizenship. These two developments intersect with each other and imply a remaking of the imagined spaces and places of citizenship from something held in common to something that is localised or specific. Contestation, then, is to be on local matters, and is to take place through managed processes of deliberation and participation, ultimately producing, it is hoped, the holy grail of the self managed community. This is unlikely to be successful as a strategy. But the double dynamic has important and troubling implications for the terrain on which publicness is contested.

Public services are deeply implicated in this double dynamic. They embody the turn to the local in an array of community endeavours, from the renaming of public libraries as community libraries or community hubs, to the devolution of (some) functions from local authorities to area or ward committees or the establishment of community health centres. But this involves having to reconcile competing views of community and of ownership in the management of these new governance spaces. At the same time, public services are also required to manage the interface between 'top down' government targets and their own wider visions and strategies, against the demands, views or choices emanating from the 'communities' they engage with or the 'customers' they are encouraged to serve on an individualised, personalised basis. The policies and strategies of New Labour have been directed towards the involvement of the public in the process of governance, either as participants in decision-making on local services or as consumers charged with driving up the performance of those services by their demands and choices.

One of the things I want to emphasise here is the increasing focus on service-specific, community or project based patterns of public engagement. Deliberative forms - citizens juries, area committees, liaison panels, senior citizens forums, user groups constituted by specific services for the purposes of consultation - all form encounters in which notions of publicness, the public interest, public value, are being negotiated around *local* or *service specific* issues in a multitude of dispersed sites. Such forums introduce the idea of recasting the public sphere around a politics of user empowerment or community participation. This is different from the turn to consumerism and choice in the current reforms of public services, but it intersects with it in important ways. Both suggest ways in which individuals and communities are being constituted as partners and collaborators in the process of governing. However both also demonstrate the possibilities of new forms of claims-making - by individuals, by user movements, and by agencies speaking in the name of the consumer. And they raise questions about the kinds of social and political imaginary being opened up and closed down in the remaking of publics. The social democratic state embodied hierarchical relationships between government and people based on liberal notions of citizenship. The remaking of publics in participative, consumerist and community locales serves to recast the public sphere as a series of horizontal spaces. Such a process is one that pervades New Labour policy documents, including a recent Demos pamphlet by Tessa Jowell on rebuilding the public sphere.[8] It is one that serves to displace the possibility of wider justice or equality claims.

Now responsive services or community engagement have to be viewed as positive rather than negative developments - but I want to highlight what happens when these strategies intersect with a different set of processes that are at stake in the remaking of publics. These involve the displacement of the 'public' with the language of the 'social': social investment, social capital, social inclusion, social cohesion and so on. In each the social is collapsed into the economic in a way that marginalises and residualises the public. This is a process whereby public investment - in infrastructure, transport, and public facilities such as libraries - has become increasingly subordinated to

8. T. Jowell, *Tackling the 'poverty of aspiration' through rebuilding the public realm*, Demos 2005.

a focus on social investment: that is, investment in the capacity of future citizens to flourish in globalised economy. Indeed the public tends to be associated with old fashioned imagery of welfare state, and with a number of public institutions (the BBC, public libraries and museums, and even the Open University) that are all associated in the Jowell paper with an historical - and now somewhat outdated - notion of a collective public sphere.

Restating the politics of the public

What I have been trying to argue is that the remaking of the public is played out around a number of different struggles. It is not one logic (privatisation) but a plurality of competing logics that create multiple spaces that social actors can engage with. However, debates about the politics of the public tend to be framed in terms of state/market binary. That is, the focus tends to be on the marketisation of goods or services previously provided by the state and/or ways in which the state can regulate or manage the market in the wider public interest. This is, of course, crucial; however, other ways in which the boundaries between notions of the public and various forms of private and personal are being remade have received rather less attention. As the title of a 2004 book suggests, the dominant response tends to be one that emphasises the importance of *Restating the State*.[9] This form of social democratic response tends to be based on a single narrative of decline (of the public sphere), and a single logic that drives it (marketisation). This is a conception that views the public sphere as spatially and temporally fixed; that locks us into a traditional notion of the public as clearly distinguished from the private; and that offers a view of the public sphere as a domain of rational deliberation that can be clearly marked from the passions and pleasures of the personal or the commercialised relationships of the market. Crucially, it also misses the gender subtext of the duality between public and private. One of the most prolific commentators on the decline of the public, David Marquand, has argued that 'if the personal is politicised, or the political personalised, the public and private domains are both likely to be twisted out of shape'.[10] This account looks back - nostalgically - to the golden days of the clarity and simplicity of class-based politics, sidelining the incursions of the social movements that brought

---

9. A. Gamble and T. Wright, T (2004) *Restating the State?*, Political Quarterly Special Issue 2004.
10. D. Marquand, *Decline of the Public: the hollowing out of citizenship*, Polity Press 2004.

new issues and agendas into the public domain. It is organised around a state/ market binary that collapses the complexity of the ways in which lives are lived, and that returns us to essentialist conceptions of individual identity and subjectivity. As such it offers a relatively narrow politics of the public sphere - one that fails to adequately acknowledge new claims for voice and justice. And it locks us into a conception of the public sphere delimited by the nation state. This then serves to sideline questions about the global impact of national policies - how, for example, the growth-based assumptions underpinning the UK policy agenda produce inequalities for 'other' publics; or how dominant UK/EU policy paradigms impact on the governance capacities of nations outside 'old' Europe.

The contradiction I set out at the beginning of this paper - how to hold on to the complexity of public and publicness while also being committed to its importance - defines the space of being able to restate a politics of the public. Rather than retelling the social democratic story of decline, I have argued for an approach that focuses on how notions of the public are being *problematised, obscured, remade and contested* through New Labour's strategies of modernisation. These are not a single project that can be collapsed in the grand narrative of neo-liberalism, nor indeed in the Giddensian story of the individuation and differentiation of 'the social' in a plural societies. Rather, they oscillate around the contradictions at the heart of the political project of New Labour - and perhaps will also be at the core of the 'neo-conservatism' of David Cameron's bright and shiny new Tory party.